❖ Traveling Together

❖ Traveling Together

A Guide for Disciple-Forming Congregations

Jeffrey D. Jones

THE
ALBAN
INSTITUTE

Herndon, Virginia
www.alban.org

The Alban Institute
2121 Cooperative Way, Suite 100
Herndon, VA 20171-3025

All scripture quotations unless otherwise noted are from the New Revised Standard Version of the Bible, copyright © 1989, Division of Christian Education of the National Council of Churches of Christ in the United States of America, and are used by permission.

Portions of Chapters 4 and 5 are revisions of material that first appeared in the "2001-2002 Christian Education Planning Guide for American Baptist Churches" and the "2002-2003 Christian Education Planning Guide for American Baptist Churches," © American Baptist Board of Education and Publication. Used by permission.

See additional permissions acknowledgements on page 205.

Cover design by Wendy Ronga, Hampton Design Group.

Library of Congress Cataloging-in-Publication Data

Jones, Jeffrey D.
  Traveling together : a guide for disciple-forming congregations / Jeffrey D. Jones.
      p. cm.
  Includes bibliographical references (p.   ).
  ISBN-13: 978-1-56699-319-7
  ISBN-10: 1-56699-319-9
  1. Discipling (Christianity) 2. Church renewal—Baptists. I. Title.
  BV4520.J56 2005
  253—dc22

                              2005030949

      09   08   07   06   05   UG   1   2   3   4   5

❖ Contents

Appendixes

❖ Foreword

THE RELIGIOUS STATUS QUO IN AMERICA TODAY IS hardly static. Until about forty years ago, it could have been said that mainline Protestantism truly was the religious mainstream. It served as the civil religion of America, politically active (in both parties), unabashedly patriotic, and confident in its traditions. Conservative evangelicals would have been a vigorous but marginal sidestream in those days—a minority by and large focused on saving souls for heaven and resisting "worldliness," generally disinterested in political power and suspicious of anything remotely resembling "the social gospel."

Now, over twice as many conservative evangelicals attend public worship on a given Sunday as mainline Protestants, and, via the Religious Right, evangelicals have become a potent force in one party of American politics—some say for better, others for worse. Today's evangelicals seem as confident in their new role as the custodians of American morals as their mainline counterparts were in the past.

After four decades of change, many mainline Protestants have begun to awaken to their new status and are moving beyond their nostalgia about the good old days and their resentment of the rise of the Religious Right. They are looking ahead with courage and hope, asking themselves what the purpose of the church should be, if not to be the custodians of national morality. They are exploring new understandings of the church and its mission, using terms like "missional" and "disciple forming" and "spiritual practice."

It's not just mainliners who are rethinking their role. In the first years of the new century, just as some evangelicals were rejoicing in their political dominance, others began having second thoughts about the exploits of the Religious Right and its widespread identification with evangelicalism. These evangelicals began to realize that the costs of partisan political involvement had been high and concluded that the gains were not worth the losses. So today, progressive evangelicals have also begun envisioning a different future than their recent trajectory—and they appear to be exploring the same territory as their progressive mainline counterparts—what it means to be missional churches, engaging in disciple formation through spiritual practices.

This parallel emergence—from the older mainline civil religion and from the newer evangelical civil religion—leads to a promising potential convergence. Jeffrey D. Jones's *Traveling Together* is the most practical exploration of this new common ground that I have seen. The book will be equally accessible to mainliners and evangelicals who wish to move beyond the cultural custodianship of civil religion to discover (and rediscover) a new (and old) missional disciple-forming identity.

I remember the conversation Jeff and I had in a little restaurant near Washington, D.C., when we talked about the possibilities of a book like this. Jeff seemed to me just the right person to take on this challenge. His background in pastoral ministry and denominational leadership, combined with his involvement with a respected mainline seminary, sensitized him to the practical requirements of disciple formation, along with the organizational realities of churches and denominations needing a fresh vision, and the needs of church leaders wishing to lead their congregations out of old ruts and into new territory.

When I read through the manuscript of the book you are now holding, I was thrilled. My expectations were high, and they were exceeded. By the time I finished Jeff's overview of Acts in chapter 2, I thought, "Wow! The first two chapters alone are more than worth the price of the book." I kept feeling the same way as I read on in chapter after chapter.

Increasing numbers of us have been talking about what a post-conservative, post-liberal convergence would look like in the American church. We have become convinced that this convergence would entail the rediscovery of the local church as a missional, disciple-making community engaged in transformative spiritual practices. *Traveling Together* beautifully conveys the vibrant possibilities before us.

But those possibilities are not guaranteed. Jeff and I both know that books are worthless unless readers like you put them into practice. Now it will be up to readers like you to experiment with the ideas and tools presented in this book to turn possibilities into actualities. When more and more of us begin launching experiments in disciple formation, and when we begin sharing our stories and learnings together, today's status quo can give way to a dynamic new reality.

Mainliners and evangelicals, writers and readers, congregational leaders and members of Christian congregations . . . we are all truly traveling together.

Brian D. McLaren

❖ Introduction

*We stand in a crisis and we can be bearers of the torch or we
can carefully husband a little flame and keep it from going out
a little longer.*

Rufus Jones

THE CRISIS OF THE MAINLINE CHURCH IN THE UNITED
States is evident. Membership is declining. Finances are precari-
ous. Denominational structures are downsizing and often consumed in controversy. Seminaries in many cases are struggling to
survive and in almost all cases are caught up in concerns about an
aging student population, curriculum revision, and the place of
traditional academic disciplines in the training of church leaders.
Conflict is a common feature of many congregations, and dissatisfaction with the pastor, the music, the youth group or any number
of other things is present in many more.

Responses to this reality have been varied. Some congregations
have hunkered down, turned inward, and developed a survival
mentality. Others have adopted strategies that have led to growth,
only to be criticized for the changes they've made and the way they
have alienated long-time members. Still others have engaged in
one after another congregational studies or adopted one after another supposed solutions, but have not yet found the approach
that can be effectively implemented in their setting. Some churches
are just dying.

The crisis is evident. It is not all doom and gloom, however. Congregations are finding new ways of being and doing church. Congregations are finding renewal and renewed vitality in worship and mission. Congregations are experiencing growth—both in numbers and in the faithfulness of their ministry. There are congregations that have responded to the crisis not by husbanding a little flame but by being bearers of a torch. This book seeks to increase the number of congregations that are torchbearers.

I believe that because of the significant cultural and societal changes that have taken place during the past several decades, virtually all the old answers about what it means to be and do church don't work anymore. This book is an attempt to respond to that reality. It asks congregations to do some hard work seeking God's will and exploring their ways. It asks for a different way of looking at what church is all about. It suggests that God's intentions for us are radically different from the ways of being and doing church with which many of us are comfortable. And yet, it also assumes that when we dig deep and begin to look with different eyes we will see things that have been there all along, that we will find new possibilities in what we thought were old answers. This crisis, as do most crises, forces us back to our roots in ways that enable us to discover what has been there all along but which we have not yet been able to see.

The book is based in three key assumptions:

1. The crisis we are in has its roots in the movement into a post-Christendom, postmodern world that has happened over the last century, but more intensely during the last 50 years.
2. In order to find its way through this crisis the church, especially the local congregation, needs to rediscover an understanding of itself as a disciple-forming community.
3. The implementation of that self-understanding has radical implications for the life, ministry, leadership, and structure of the church.

I have written this book with the intention that it will be helpful for anyone who has an interest in and concern for the life and ministry of the church, who has a sense that things are not what they might be, and who is seeking a new understanding of congregational life and mission. In most cases these will be leaders in the church; many of them will not be ordained. While the book discusses biblical and theological concepts and insights, it does not assume a high level of expertise in these areas. In tandem with my three assumptions, this book will:

1. Discuss key features of the post-Christendom, postmodern world and their meaning for congregations
2. Present a framework for discipleship along with a rationale for this framework being the foundation for a congregation's life and mission
3. Suggest implications of the discipleship framework for eight key areas in the life and leadership of the congregation

I developed the concepts central to the book over the past 20 years, while serving both as a pastor and a national denominational staff member. They are a product of those experiences, of the insight provided by others (both in writing and in personal conversation), and the more intensive study opportunity offered through involvement in the Doctor of Ministry program at Andover Newton Theological School. The concepts have been tested in discussions with those who worked with me and in workshops I have led with participants who represented significant racial/ethnic, geographic, educational, economic, and theological diversity. Additionally, the concept of the congregation as a disciple-forming community, the elements of discipleship, and the characteristics of disciple-forming congregations that are central to the project were tested in three focus groups (in California, Indiana, and Massachusetts). The feedback and suggestions received in those settings affirmed the basic concepts of the book and provided both insight and encouragement. The idea of a guide grew out of a conversation with Brian McLaren, who encouraged me to develop a resource that could be read and used by a wide range of people in a congregation. The current format results from helpful suggestions made by Tom Bandy regarding the areas of concern that were most significant.

In particular I would like to thank the following people for their helpful participation in the process. Those I worked with as the concepts began to take concrete form and who helped shape them in many significant ways: Brad Berglund, Yvonne Carter, Mayra Castañeda, Becky Crouch, Lynne Eckman, and Thom Son. Those who have read and offered suggestions of various drafts: Dean Allen, Lowell Fewster, Alan Newton, Robert Pazmiño, and Jeff Woods. Those who have provided encouragement, a listening ear, and a strong shoulder along the way and whose questions and concerns continually pushed me to probe more deeply: Jim Cummings, Tripp Dixon, and Andy Samson. And Kristy Pullen, with whom I have both suffered and celebrated in the past several years and who, in the surprising grace of God, has been both advocate for and editor of this manuscript.

Most of all thanks beyond words go to my wife, Judy, who continues to evidence all the fruits of the Spirit in her relationship with me.

PREPARING FOR THE JOURNEY

As you read this introduction we start out on a long road together. At the very least, it will be a journey. But if things go well and we do it in the right spirit, it will be a pilgrimage—a journey with a sacred purpose. What could be more sacred than attending to the question of what God wants us to be and do? And that is what this book is about. Our focus is what God wants us to be and do, both as individuals and as the church. Our destination is to become the church God is calling us to be.

Think about this book as a guide for our journey/pilgrimage. It will alert us to the pleasures and dangers along the road and help us understand a bit more fully how things got to be the way they are. It points out the sights, tells us about the good and bad things to be alert for, and provides some helpful background. It doesn't tell you precisely what to do, what route to take. You'll have to do that part on your own. It isn't a roadmap. But like most guidebooks, once you've read it, deciding on the specific route will be easier and the route you plan will be better geared to what you want the journey to be about, where you want the journey to lead.

As thorough as guidebooks are, they don't tell you about everything you will encounter. This book doesn't do that either—it would be too long if it tried. But more importantly, the attempt to do that would be an impossible one. No one can anticipate what you will encounter along the way. Some of it you will simply need to improvise on the fly.

Also like most guidebooks, this one will probably paint a less than fully accurate picture of reality. Part of that is certainly because reality can never be captured on paper. Another part is that we all see things differently. I can remember a number of times when the glowing descriptions of a place led me to find it while traveling, only to be greatly disappointed by what I actually saw. Maybe the sun was in a different place so the light was different; maybe things had changed since the writer had been there; maybe her taste was different from mine. Whatever the reason, I ended up being disappointed. As long as it didn't happen consistently, however, it didn't lessen my trust in the guidebook. You may very likely have a similar experience on the journey you take with this book. Things won't appear to you the way I describe them. But hopefully there will be enough accuracy and enough consistency for you to continue to trust the guidebook!

Without pushing this guidebook metaphor further than is reasonable, there is one more important analogy I'd like to make. You rarely read a guidebook from cover to cover. In fact, most guidebooks are simply not written to be read that way. You have that same kind of freedom in reading this book as well. There are any number of places you could begin. It is quite possible to come back to earlier chapters after you've read later ones or to skip some chapters altogether. You can, of course, read the book straight through from front to back, but here are some suggestions for how to do it differently, based on particular interests you might have:

+ If you want a better understanding of some of the issues that led me to begin this journey, start with chapter 1. This chapter looks at some of the reasons why it is so difficult to "do" church these days. If you want to probe these reasons more fully, skip from chapter 1 to chapter 9, which explores the decline of Christendom and the demise of the modern age in more detail and considers some of the implications for the church.

+ If you would like to get a grasp of biblical foundations for understanding the purpose of the church, begin with chapter 2, which looks at the ministry of Jesus and the life of the early church in order to gain insights into what it means to be a follower of Jesus.

+ If you want to look at what it means for an individual person to live as a disciple in today's world, begin with chapter 3. In this chapter we look at discipleship as a way to think about our core reason for being.

+ If you want to consider the key experiences that contribute to the growth of disciples, begin with chapters 4 and 5, which describe three elements of discipleship and the practices of the church that form disciples by enabling them to experience these elements.

+ If you want get right to the changes that need to happen in a church in order for it to help disciples grow, begin with chapter 6. In this chapter we look at eight important qualities of a disciple-forming congregation.

+ If you would like to explore a biblical time that has many similarities to our own and see what we can learn from it, begin with chapter 10. This chapter draws parallels between our experience and the experience of the Israelites in exile in Babylon.

You can begin with any of these chapters and pick up the other ones along the journey to fill in needed information or help you flesh out ideas that are beginning to form. The important thing is to begin at a point that interests you. Some people like to get right to the practical, so chapters 3, 4, 5 and 6 will interest them more. Other people like to understand the background and the concepts that shape the practical. They should begin with chapter 1, 9 or 10. With a regular guidebook you read about the city you're in first and go from there. With this guidebook, read about what interests you first and go from there. I, of course, have a personal hope that you will read the entire book in some order, but how you do that is very much up to you!

My greater hope, however, is that in some way this guidebook will help turn the journey you are on into a pilgrimage. It is not easy to be the congregation God wants us to be. I believe one way to do that is to rediscover the importance of discipleship—of reclaiming the call to be disciple-forming communities. That will require effort; it will demand boldness; it will almost inevitably result in conflict. In the midst of all of that, I hope this book can help you stay focused on where you are and why, as well as on where you want to be and how. If it does that, pilgrimage is possible!

❖

My own journey into more faithful discipleship began before I can remember. A family of faith, a community of faith, and friends of faith nurtured me early in my life. It was in seminary, however, that I had my first experience providing leadership in an intentional faith community. I went off to seminary knowing one thing with absolute certainty: there was no way in the world I would ever spend my Sunday evenings babysitting a bunch of bratty senior high youth! God had another idea, however, and it wasn't more than three weeks before I was working with a senior high youth group in a church not far from the school. Each Sunday night when my friends and I would get back to campus we'd go out to eat and tell the stories of our weekend. They would talk about all the exciting and creative things their youth groups had done. I would say nothing. For, you see, the kids in my youth group were there largely because they didn't belong anyplace else. They weren't creative or talented. No great enthusiasm was generated when we came together. More often than not it was a challenge just to get them to talk. I planned programs galore. We did things, viewed things, went places together, but still nothing great happened. I was bemoaning my plight one day, when a wise professor told me perhaps the most important thing I learned in seminary. He said something like this: "If you believe God is at work in the lives of these youth, if you believe God is present among you, then all you need to do is live with them and try to be constantly attentive to the presence of God. And it will happen." He was right.

Sometime during our second year together little splashes of creativity began to happen. One girl took guitar lessons and we began to sing together. Several group members grew concerned about a number of social issues that were significant at the time and we began to talk about them and then do something about them. They began to invite their friends to join the group, because they sensed something important was happening and they wanted others to experience it. By the third year this dull and boring group of nobodies had become one of the most exciting, alive, creative, enthusiastic groups of people I have ever known.

Along the way, many people offered explanations of this experience. Some attributed it to the enthusiasm of youth—willing to try knew things, grow, change, become something different—with the clear implication being that this kind of thing doesn't happen with adults. Others, more sophisticated in their analysis, said the key issue at work here was adolescent identity formation; youth were trying on new identities to see which one fit and I just happened to catch this group at the point they were trying on this identity. A different group acknowledged the wonder of such an experience, but quickly followed it up by telling me that things like this didn't happen very often in the church and I would certainly be disappointed if I expected them to. I decided not to believe any of them.

What I believe was at work in that group was nothing less than the transforming power of the gospel of Jesus Christ. I believe that this is what God intends for everyone—children, youth, and adults—all the time. I believe this is what the church is supposed to be like—all the time. I believe that when a church is what God wants it to be, this is what happens—all the time. I believe that this is what being a disciple-forming church is all about.

One ❖ Where Are We?

It was sometime in 1993 that I finally verbalized a thought that had been gradually forming in my mind for a number of years. I just blurted it out in the middle of a church board meeting. When I said it, board members were taken back. I was shocked. Since then, however, that statement has shaped both my study and practice of ministry. The statement I made that fateful night was: virtually all the old answers about what it means to be and do church don't work any more.

Perhaps you have sensed it, too. Boards continue to meet. They continue to plan programs—good programs. Worship continues in the established patterns of the past years—the music is as good as ever; the quality of the sermons hasn't declined. You're still offering a high-quality graded Sunday school for children at all levels. Maybe the congregation has made some adaptations to better respond to the realities it is facing. Perhaps you've reduced the length of terms on boards to two years from three because you found that people did not want to make long-term commitments. Perhaps you've added more contemporary music to the worship service or even established a "seeker service." Perhaps you've changed the

Sunday school curriculum in order to make it more teacher-friendly or activity-based. But somehow something is missing. It's still difficult to recruit the board members. Worship attendance has hit a plateau or is declining. More and more it seems like you're just going through the motions. You're doing what you know how to do. You're doing what has always worked before. But now, it just doesn't seem to be working. And you wonder what's wrong—what's wrong with the church, with the people, with the leaders, with yourself.

That's what I had been struggling with for a number of years in two different churches. And yet more and more I found it all but impossible to avoid thinking that I was just "playing pastor"—doing the things I had been taught to do in seminary and by my mentors, keeping the organization running, leading meaningful worship, planning interesting programs. Yes, more and more it seemed to me that I was simply going through the motions and it just wasn't enough any more. I could literally feel the energy draining from my body and the congregational body. I knew something different was needed, but I didn't know what. When I spoke those words that evening they really surprised me. I had never said them before, even to myself. I had never put it that way before, even in my private thoughts. All the old answers about what it means to do and be church don't work any more. I'd said it at last. Now, what could I do with it?

First of all, I knew I needed to have some sense of why that was true. Why didn't the old answers work anymore? Why did doing the things I had been trained to do and could do well seem more and more like going through the motions? Why was it so hard to get things to work the way I knew they were supposed to work, so that we could really be the church that God had called us to be?

When I looked around me with that question in mind I began to see things that might provide the beginning of an answer:

- My sons' soccer teams regularly scheduled games on Sunday morning.
- Even though the town I was a pastor in started out as a Methodist camp meeting and continued to have a large number of churches, more and more people seemed to use Sunday as the day to sleep in.

- One of my sons did his homework while listening to the radio, surfing the net, instant messaging his friends, and watching a TV program with the sound turned off—all at the same time.
- Shopping malls were open on Sundays and did a great business on Sunday mornings.
- In the national media I was hearing more and more conversation about the possibility of taxing churches.
- Racial, ethnic, and religious diversity was becoming more and more obvious as an everyday experience.
- Companies were downsizing and restructuring—changing in all sorts of ways to respond to what they saw as new business realities.

What all of this began to say to me was that some significant changes were taking place in the world. What seemed obvious and commonplace for me as I was growing up was no longer the reality I was facing in my daily life. It was hard to estimate the extent of these changes, but they seemed significant. More and more it seemed as though it was these changes that were the most important factor in the reality I was facing. If the old answers didn't work any more it was because the world in which they had worked was no more. A new world had dawned and new answers were needed for that world.

Over the years the radical nature of the changes has become more apparent. On a personal level I've encountered realities such as these:

- My older son met his first girlfriend, who lives in Tokyo, while they were studying in China.
- My younger son, before he had graduated from college, had studied in England and China and traveled throughout most of eastern Europe.
- The denominational agency I spent 15 years of my ministry working with has gone out of existence.
- Congregations and denominations are almost without exception facing severe financial challenges.

And so it goes. Something extremely significant is happening in the world and in churches. Profound changes are taking place.

As I looked further into the nature of these changes I discovered two factors that most people think are of great significance: the decline of Christendom and the demise of modernity. We don't need to go into these in great depth at this point. If you want to explore these phenomena more fully, chapter 9 will help you do that. For now, let's simply look quickly at them so we have a better sense of some of the reasons they have helped create a situation in which the old answers don't work any more.

For the first three centuries of its existence the Christian church existed on the fringes of society. It was a minority group, proclaiming a faith that seemed strange by almost any prevailing standard. That all ended in 313, when Constantine proclaimed Christianity the official religion of the Empire. Over the years since then Christianity has been involved in a complex relationship with government and society—each supporting the aims of the other, while also using the other for its purposes. This relationship has taken many forms during that time, but it has almost always meant that the church could rely on cultural support for its beliefs and practices. Sometimes this happened through a direct alliance of church and state, supported by governmental edict. At other times it happened more subtly, but still effectively. For example, in the United States there were blue laws to limit conflicts with Sunday worship and the daily recitation of the Lord's Prayer in many schools. Beyond those, however, additional cultural support for the practice of Christianity came in an attitudinal assumption that being part of a church was the right thing to do. It was the way you provided your children the nurture they needed. It was the way in which you served your community. It was the place you could make the connections that would enhance your career. Taken together, all of these factors (and many more) provided an environment in which the church could count on a steady source of members, simply because being a church member was the thing to do.

That is no longer the case. The decline of Christendom has meant that the various cultural supports for Christian beliefs and practices have disappeared. There are numerous reasons for that. Part of it is the growing number of other faiths that are now practiced in the United States. Part of it is that the increased secularization of society has meant that people have looked to places other than the church to provide for their needs. Part of it is the simple reality that because *not* going to church is now an acceptable way of life, many of the advantages that used to adhere to church membership no longer do so. In short, the decline of Christendom has meant that there is no longer any strong cultural support for practices that encouraged church attendance. In a very real sense, the church is now left to itself to reach and involve people; it can no longer rely on cultural forces to do that.

The demise of modernity is the second key element of our changing world. The modern worldview no longer has the power to shape our life and living. Its belief in the possibility of truly objective truth, in the supremacy of logical thought, and in the inevitability of progress is being questioned and rejected on almost every front. There is a deeper understanding of the importance of one's context in shaping an understanding of reality and truth. There is suspicion of those people and institutions that assume they are possessors of a truth that is valid for everyone and seek to impose that truth on others.

The reality of this postmodern mindset was brought powerfully home to me when my family and I were looking for a new church to attend. As we went through this search we would attend churches for several weeks and talk about our experiences, mainly in worship. My younger son was still living at home at the time. He is the one I mentioned earlier, who studied while listening to the stereo, watching TV, surfing the net, and instant messaging his friends. When I began to look at a typical worship service through his eyes, I realized how alien it must be to him—to say nothing of boring! For the worship I grew up with, the worship I led as a pastor, and the worship we were attending were invariably linear, with one thing following another. It was overwhelmingly cerebral and logic-based. It contained none of the elements that were a part of his daily experience, part of his environment, his way of communicating and learning. One Sunday I realized that, apart from two illustrations in the sermon, the entire worship service could just as easily have occurred in the 1930s as the 1990s. And even if there had been some contemporary music thrown in, it still would not have resonated with the experiences of his living. When we talk about the demise of modernity and the emergence of post-modernity, this is what we are talking about.

Even though the postmodern world is radically different from the one in which I grew up and with which I am most familiar, there is much about it that intrigues me. The rejection of logic as the final determiner of truth, for example, has opened the door for a new appreciation of mystery and of the spiritual dimension of life. That creates a setting in which the work of the Spirit in our lives can be recognized and appreciated in new ways. The openness to diversity that comes as a part of understanding the importance of context can lead us into new experiences of learning and growing together with others.

The more I looked at it the more I began to understand that these broader changes taking place in the world were the key to understanding why the old answers didn't work any more. It wasn't that I wasn't as capable or faithful as some previous pastor. It wasn't that the members of the congregation weren't committed or that young people didn't care. Once we accepted that reality we could move beyond the very natural tendency to find someone to blame for our sorry situation. Instead we could begin to consider together what we might do about it.

It is important for us to bring a faith perspective to this discussion. What is God up to in all of this? What is happening through the challenge to old understandings of the church brought upon by our post-Christendom, postmodern world? I continued to wrestle with those questions and they led to even more questions. Could it be that the church itself has become too reliant on someone else, namely the state, to further its teachings and values and to provide its members? Could it be that the church has become so much a product of the age that it has lost a clear sense of its own unique role and purpose? Such a church is a church in name only. It is a church without passion or purpose. God would surely have little patience with such a church. God would certainly want to shake such a church out of its complacency. If we can bring that perspective to our understanding of our post-Christendom, postmodern world, then we need to be open to the possibility that the struggles of these times are God's way of calling the church to be what it is supposed to be, to do what it is supposed to do in this new world. Maybe that is why the old answers don't work any more. Maybe this is God's way of telling us that it is time to take our faith deeper. Maybe in this time God is offering us a great opportunity to discover anew what God has called the church to be, a chance to take on the challenge of seeking God's new church and actually helping to shape it.

❖

　All of this explains how I came to write this book. If the old answers don't work anymore, and if at least part of the reason for this is the world in which those answers did work no longer exists, then what are we to do about it? How do we discover anew what it means to be a church so that we can begin to develop answers that do work? Or, in the words of Psalm 137, how can we sing the Lord's song in a foreign land?

In many ways this book describes my journey of discovering the answers to those questions. But its focus isn't my journey. It's yours. I'll try to act as your guide along the way. I'll take you to the places that have been interesting ones for me, I'll point out the things I've noticed and share some of my own experiences. But our focus will always be on your experience, not mine. I'll encourage you to make your own discoveries, to see things I didn't see, and to put it all together in a way that it becomes your own.

When I'm surrounded by the new, when I've lost my bearings and don't know which way to turn, I search out something—anything—that is familiar. More specifically, something of substance that is familiar. Something I can hang on to. Something that will give me solid ground on which to stand when all around seems to be sinking sand. In my journey of faith, that something has always been the Bible. And so that is where I turned first in my attempt to find the new answers. That is where our journey will begin as well.

In the Bible Abraham and Sarah were the first to receive God's promise of a new land (Genesis 12). In order to begin to live out of that promise they needed to leave the comfort of home and journey into the unknown. We are very much like them—setting out not knowing where we are going (Hebrews 11:8). Like them, we need to be guided by faith, trusting in God, believing that God is present and at work even when we do not understand. Like them, we will undoubtedly laugh at some of the things God says to us along the way—laugh, not because it is so funny, but because we believe we cannot conceive it (Genesis 17:25–27; 18:1–15). Like them, we probably will never arrive at the land that God has in mind for us—at least not in this earthly life. But like them, journey we must, for that is what it means to be faithful.

Two ❖ Back to the Basics

W E ARE LIVING IN A TIME OF PROFOUND CHANGE. Our challenge in this time is to discover the ways in which we ourselves need to change in order to adjust to the new realities of our world. We cannot keep doing things the way we have always done them. But neither will it do us any good to simply change for the sake of change or to jump on the bandwagon of the newest fad of a fickle world. In times of great change, in times when the old answers just don't seem to work any more, the most important thing we can do is to go back to our roots. This doesn't mean keep doing what we have been doing, for in most cases that isn't our roots at all, just old branches. It is the way we had accommodated to changes we faced sometime in the past. Our roots go deeper than that—in both time and meaning. For Christians, those roots are discovered in the Bible, most especially in the New Testament.

In this chapter we will take a look at those roots, to see what they tell us about what is most important. We'll begin by reminding ourselves what Jesus said we should be about, both as individual Christians and as a church.

THE MINISTRY OF JESUS

Jesus' public ministry began with his baptism (Luke 3:21–22). This was followed by a time of personal testing and discernment in the wilderness temptation (Luke 4:1–13). "Then Jesus, filled with the power of the Spirit, returned to Galilee, and a report about him spread through all the surrounding country. He began to teach in their synagogues and was praised by everyone" (Luke 4:14–15). This praise soon turned to scorn, however, for his teaching in his own hometown of Nazareth so angered the people that they wanted to kill him (Luke 4:16–30). Following this rejection of his teaching Jesus' healing ministry begins (Luke 4:31–41). His popularity is great, his ministry is significant, he is filled with the power of the Spirit, and he has a clear sense of being about the work God sent him to do. But still Jesus understands that something more is needed. He goes off to a lonely place to pray and, perhaps in this time, makes what will prove to be a momentous decision. The next thing Luke tells us is that Jesus began to call others to be with him (Luke 5:1–11). From this point on the story is not just about Jesus; it is about Jesus and his disciples.

Let's stop here a minute and reflect on the insights that come from just this small portion of Luke's Gospel. In it we see:

+ Baptism is the marker that sets a person apart for a special way of living; testing and discernment are needed in order to be about God's work.
+ The Spirit's presence empowers for ministry.
+ Doing God's work provokes praise in some and anger in others.
+ Both teaching and healing (talking and doing) are important to ministry.
+ Ministry happens in both the synagogue and in the world.
+ Being with others who share your sense of call is essential.

How might these insights shape the way we go about being and doing church in today's world? That's a question to keep in mind as we continue to look at the ministry of Jesus with his disciples.

Not even Jesus was a Lone Ranger. He understood the importance—the absolute necessity, really—of being part of a community in which he could share his faith and ministry. So Jesus brought together a group of diverse people who had a common commitment. In their life together they learned more about Jesus, his call, and his ministry. They faced the joys and challenges of ministry. They grew in their own faith and their understanding of God's will, both for them and for all creation. In their life together, as they learned more about Jesus and shared in his ministry, they began to be formed as his disciples.

There was for this community a rhythm of involvement and retreat, of ministry and reflection. They were with Jesus as he taught and healed and cast out demons; they witnessed his responses to the challenges from the religious authorities. They were constantly on the move. And yet there were also times of rest and quiet, when the active life of ministering was put on hold for a while. There was time to ask Jesus questions about what they were doing (Luke 8:9, 9:49–50, 11:1, 12:41). There was time for Jesus to talk with them about what it meant to be a disciple (Luke 9:21–27, 12:22–31, 17:1–6). There was time to pray together (Luke 9:18, 9:28). There were times when the failure of the disciples provided the opportunity for Jesus to teach them even more (Luke 8:22–25, 9:12–17, 9:46–48, 18:15–17). In all of this the purpose was for them to go deeper in their own faith, to grow in their ability to serve others, and to be engaged in God's mission.

This is a community of faith. It is, as is the church, a community that has come together around Jesus. For the disciples, and for us as we read their story, Jesus is the model for our discipleship. He teaches us what we are to be about and he shows us. When the teaching and showing come together, the most profound learning about being a disciple of Jesus takes place.

To be a disciple of Jesus is to be on a journey. Jesus led his disciples on a journey that was both physical and spiritual. They traveled throughout Galilee to share the good news of God's kingdom with as many people as possible. They traveled to Jerusalem to fulfill God's plan for Jesus' own death and resurrection. And he taught them: "Foxes have holes, and birds of the air have nests; but the Son of Man has nowhere to lay his head" (Luke 9:58).

To be a disciple of Jesus is to serve others. Jesus spent his ministry caring for the needs of others—healing and casting out demons so that they would experience health and wholeness, giving himself so that sins could be forgiven. At his last meal with his disciples, Jesus washed their feet (John 13:2–17). And he taught them: "Whoever wants to be first must be last of all and servant of all" (Mark 9:35).

To be a disciple of Jesus is to be obedient to God in all things. Jesus went to the cross in obedience to God, saying, "not my will but yours be done" (Luke 22:42). And he taught them: "Whoever does the will of God is my brother and sister and mother" (Mark 3:35).

To be a disciple of Jesus is to make God's work the highest priority in our lives. Jesus left his own family and withstood temptations to personal comfort, power, and glory (Luke 4:1–13). And he taught them: "No one who puts a hand to the plow and looks back is fit for the kingdom of God" (Luke 9:62).

To be a disciple of Jesus is to pray. In the midst of all the demands of his ministry, Jesus consistently found time to be in prayer—both alone and with others (Matthew 14:23, 19:13, 26:36; Luke 6:12. 9:28). And he taught them: "Whatever you ask for in prayer with faith, you will receive" (Matthew 21:22).

To be a disciple of Jesus is to live with the conviction that love of God and love of people are intimately tied together. Jesus demonstrated his love of God in his passionate following of God's will; he demonstrated his love of people in his compassionate response to their needs. And he taught them: "The first [commandment] is, 'Hear, O Israel: the Lord our God, the Lord is one; you shall love the Lord your God with all your heart, and with all your soul, and with all your mind, and with all your strength.' The second is this, 'You shall love your neighbor as yourself.' There is no other commandment greater than these" (Mark 12:29–31).

To be a disciple of Jesus is to show concern for the outcasts of society. Jesus dined with tax collectors and sinners, despite the scorn of others. And he taught them: "Truly I tell you, just as you did it to one of the least of these who are members of my family, you did it to me . . .. Truly I tell you, just as you did not do it to one of the least of these, you did not do it to me" (Matthew 25:40, 45).

To be a disciple of Jesus is sometimes to suffer. Jesus was stripped, beaten, mocked, and crucified. And he taught them: "If any want to become my followers, let them deny themselves and take up their cross daily and follow me. For those who want to save their life will lose it, and those who lose their life for my sake will save it" (Luke 9:23–24).

To be a disciple of Jesus is to live by different rules. Jesus healed and ate on the Sabbath, despite the protestations of the good religious people of his day. And he taught them: "You have heard that it was said . . . . But I say to you . . . ." (Matthew 5:21, 22; 27, 28; 31, 32; 33, 34; 38, 39; 43, 44).

To be a disciple of Jesus is to have faith. Jesus lived and died with faith in the love and purpose of God. And he taught them: "For truly I tell you, if you have faith the size of a mustard seed, you will say to this mountain, 'Move from here to there,' and it will move; and nothing will be impossible for you" (Matthew 17:20–21).

To be a disciple of Jesus is to continue his work of ministry. Jesus sent the disciples into ministry (Luke 9:1–6). And he taught them: "Very truly, I tell you, the one who believes in me will also do the works that I do and, in fact, will do greater works than these, because I am going to the Father" (John 14:12).

This is what Jesus taught about following him to those he gathered around him. At times those disciples didn't appear to be very good learners. Especially in Mark's Gospel, they are pictured as a pretty dense group of people, unable to grasp what Jesus is trying to teach them. When he first told them of his impending suffering and death, Peter rebuked him for saying such a thing (Mark 8:31–33). When he told them a second time, they simply didn't understand what he was talking about, but were afraid to ask him what he meant (Mark 9:30–32). And later, after he told them the third time, James and John came to him with a request to sit beside him on his throne of glory—seemingly oblivious to the suffering that Jesus had talked about. When the other disciples heard of their request it sparked a jealous argument (Mark 10:32–45). Time and time again Jesus wondered about the faith of the disciples: when they were caught in a storm on the lake (Mark 4:35–41); when Peter was unable to walk to him on the water (Matthew 14:22–32); when they had no bread to eat (Matthew 16:5–12); when they worried (Luke 12:22–29). In the end, when he faced his greatest trial, his most trusted disciples fell asleep on him (Mark 14:32–42), one of them betrayed him (Mark 14:43–47), all of them deserted him (Mark 14:50), and the most loyal one denied him (Mark 14:66–72). And yet, it is to these people that Jesus entrusted the future of his ministry. Despite their slowness to understand, despite their seeming inability to grasp the message, despite their doubts and mistakes and pettiness, Jesus commissioned them to be his witnesses to the world (Matthew 28:16–20; Luke 24:45–49). Disciples, it seems, do not have to be perfect—in either the understanding or the practice of their faith. What they do need is to be devoted to Jesus, eager to grow in relationship with him, and willing to be his witnesses to the world.

A. B. Bruce, the nineteenth century author of a classic description of the discipling relationship between Jesus and his disciples, in writing about Peter, Andrew, James, and John, might well have been describing all the original disciples, as well as those who have followed them:

> With all their imperfections, which were both numerous and great, these humble fishermen of Galilee had, at the very outset of their career one grand distinguishing virtue, which, though it may coexist with many defects, is the certain forerunner of ultimate high attainment. They were animated by a devotion to Jesus and to the divine kingdom. Which made them capable of any sacrifice."[1]

There is one other aspect of the ministry of Jesus we need to consider at this point. That is his relationship with the Pharisees. Clearly, this was radically different from his relationship with the disciples. The Gospels are filled with passages that portray the Pharisees in a bad light. They opposed Jesus. Jesus criticized them. The image we are left with, at least the one we have come to accept, is of a group of people who were self-righteous nitpickers, utterly lacking in humility and eager to show off their own goodness while they condemn others for failing to live up to their hard-hearted legalisms. That, however, is not the true picture of the Pharisees. In fact, when we see them in a more accurate light, we will recognize a number of similarities with ourselves. Then, Jesus' words to them begin to take on a new meaning for us.

The Pharisees were one of a number of sects or movements in the Judaism of Jesus' day. They were, by most accounts, the one most attuned to the people and most concerned to make their faith a matter of everyday life.[2] They, as most Jews, were concerned with holiness: how was it possible to attain the holiness to which God called them? The Pharisees answered this question in a way that was significantly different from the Sadducees and Essenes, two other contemporary movements. The Sadducees believed that this holiness was to be found in the temple and its worship. The Essenes believed it could be found in the ascetic community, removed from worldly concerns and pursuits. The Pharisees, in contrast, sought to make this holiness available to everyone. Their focus on the Law was a way to "democratize" holiness by making it possible for anyone to live a holy life, even as they continued in their normal pursuits. The Pharisees were primarily a movement of the laity, reducing the role of the temple priesthood in the practice of their faith. Because they believed in the importance of the oral tradition in shaping both belief and practice, the Pharisees also adopted beliefs, such as the resurrection, that were not clearly stated in the Torah. In this they stood in sharp contrast to the Sadducees, who were much more rigid, far less open.

If in fact the Pharisees were the more open, less rigid, more democratic, less conservative of the Jews, if they took their faith seriously and sought to apply it to their everyday lives, why did Jesus have such a great problem with them?

There were undoubtedly rigid, hypocritical and self-righteous people among the Pharisees, just as there certainly are among those who call themselves Christians today. Jesus' criticism of them is understandable, even in the strong language he sometimes used, such as calling them a "brood of vipers." (Matthew 12:34). Additionally, it is important to recognize that one of the reasons there was more conflict with the Pharisees than with other sects is that the Pharisees had more in common with the followers of Jesus than did others. Because of these commonalities, the differences became more important. His teachings could not simply be dismissed as belonging to someone who was so far off base that what he said and did didn't really matter.

Beyond these, we can point to several qualities of the Pharisees that might well have been the source of conflict.

Like most noble efforts, the Pharisees' focus on the Law as the way to holiness could easily be taken to extremes. What was good about it was that it allowed faith to be practiced outside the temple and apart from the priests. Because it required strict adherence to the law, however, it became rigid. Even attempts to lessen the rigidity by allowing exceptions only increased the problem of an unruly set of regulations. In the midst of all of this, it was easy to become focused on the incidentals and forget the essence. This is the basis for one of Jesus' strongest condemnations of the Pharisees: "You blind guides! You strain out a gnat but swallow a camel!" (Matthew 23:24). Before we jump on the bandwagon of criticism, however, it would be well for us to think about the arguments so many churches have over the kind of music that will be used in worship. A helpful question for us to ask in our attempt to keep our priorities in better order than the Pharisees might be: did Jesus die for this?

The focus of the Pharisees on holiness, even though they handled it better than others, also created barriers to relationship. Many of Jesus' parables deal with this issue. In the parable of the Pharisee and the Publican (Luke 18:10–14), for example, although the prayers of thanksgiving offered by the Pharisee are genuine, they serve to separate him from the tax collector, whom he looks down on for not meeting the standards of holiness he believes are appropriate. Who wouldn't be pleased that God had not made him a thief and a traitor to his people? Who wouldn't be happy that God had enabled him to live a life that made holiness possible? The Pharisee thanked God for these things, acknowledging that it was God that was responsible. That's not the problem. The issue here is that he allows his own goodness to create a barrier between him and others. His goodness undercuts his relationships, with people and ultimately with God. The same dynamic is at work in the older brother in the parable of the prodigal son. His goodness creates a barrier between him and his brother. He cannot even acknowledge him as a brother, but calls him "this son of yours" (Luke 15:30). Again, it is important for us to stop and think. Are there ways in which our goodness (something that we should and do cherish) creates barriers between others and ourselves? If people do not act or dress or talk as we think appropriate, are we less likely to relate to them, less likely to welcome them in our church?

While there were exceptions, for the Pharisees as a group holiness had become more important than humility, rules had become more important than relationship, piety had become more important than people. These are characteristics not entirely foreign to many churches. Kathleen Kern puts it starkly: "The average Pharisee was no more hardhearted, unloving, or hypocritical than the average churchgoing North American. Members of both groups felt strongly about their beliefs. Both were intensely concerned about pleasing God. Both could become so caught up in the details of their religious life that they could forget or ignore the real presence of God in the lives."[3]

I believe it would be a helpful exercise for all of us who seek to be disciples of Jesus every now and then to read the Gospels as if we are the Pharisees. We are the good, religious folk who take our religion seriously. We are the ones who have created and follow a whole array of practices that we use to determine the level of our own and others' commitment. We are the ones who too often let our goodness separate us from the people who most need Jesus. We are the ones who have reduced dynamic relationship to ritualistic habit, living faithfully to acting nicely, laying down our lives to lying down to rest. To read the Gospels as if we were the Pharisees is to let Jesus offend us and challenge us and call us to repent. To read the Gospels as if we were the Pharisees is also to let Jesus invite us to new life. Every now and then we need to read the Gospels as though we were the Pharisees. For sometimes and in some ways we are!

The Life of the Early Church

Our look at the life of the early church is focused on the book of Acts. Rather than discuss broad insights, as we did in our look at the ministry of Jesus, our approach here will be to consider specific passages in order to discover the meaning they might have for congregations today. As we do that our primary concern will be to let the passages raise questions for us about our own discipleship and the life of our congregations. Before we begin, however, let's remind ourselves why this is a helpful exercise.

It is helpful, in the first place, because the Bible and its insights are of primary interest for us whenever we want to consider what it means to be disciples or what it means to be a church. Baptists, who are a non-creedal people, talk about the Bible as "the sole rule of faith and practice." Even those who recognize an important role for creeds and church doctrine, however, turn to the Bible with special reverence and take its insights with utmost seriousness.

It is helpful, secondly, because in Acts we have the story of the very first church. This was a group that wasn't shaped by the way it had always been done and therefore was more open to discovering the best way to do it. Certainly there were times, as in the disputes between Jewish and Gentile Christians, when tradition played an important role and had to be considered. But there is in Acts a picture of a church "starting from scratch" that makes it a great learning laboratory for us. Robert Wall reminds us in his commentary on Acts: "With each new conflict, external or internal, the apostles are forced to discern afresh the ways of Israel's God and to call the emerging church back to worship and to reliance on the spiritual resources God has made available to them."[4]

It is helpful, additionally, because the situation of the early church bears many similarities to that of today's church. It was in an alien culture that accorded it few privileges and was, in many cases, suspicious of what the church was all about. That is perhaps more similar to our own situation than we are comfortable admitting. It is clear from our discussion in chapter 1, however, that the culture in which the church finds itself today is far less supportive than in the recent past. In looking at the ways in which the early church dealt with a similar situation there is much that we can learn.

It would be best for you to read each Bible passage before reading the section related to it. That way you will encounter the Word directly. Perhaps the passages will speak to you in different ways, for there is far more richness in them than can possibly be contained in these brief comments. Let's begin!

Acts 1:6–10. When the time came for Jesus to be taken into heaven he went with his disciples to a hill outside Jerusalem. There, knowing that something of profound significance was about to happen, they asked him one more question: "Lord, is this the time you will restore the kingdom to Israel?" Avoiding any commitment to a timeframe, but assuring them that they would receive the power to be his witnesses, Jesus ascended into heaven. The disciples, as anyone would expect, simply stood there in amazement, staring toward heaven. Suddenly two men in white robes appeared and asked, "Men of Galilee, why do you stand looking up toward heaven?" Following assurances that Jesus would return in the same way he had ascended, the disciples journeyed back to Jerusalem to await the gift of power that Jesus promised.

While biblical scholars debate the precise meaning of the disciples' question,[5] one intriguing aspect of it is the language that is used. The framework for the disciples is still the nation of Israel and God's special relationship with it. They are not yet able to talk about the church, the new thing God is doing. It might well be that God is always one step ahead of us, doing the new thing while we are still caught in the framework of the old. Jesus' instruction to the disciples in this situation is to wait, wait until a new power is given to them. This wasn't "twiddling the thumbs" waiting, but active waiting through prayer. It wasn't just standing there staring up into heaven, but actively seeking God's promised gift.

The church is to be a community that encourages actively seeking God's new thing so that the old ways of thinking and doing can be set aside.

A question to consider: are we willing to set aside old notions of how Jesus is at work and focus on discovering what it means to be his witnesses now?

Acts 2:1–13. The disciples did not need to wait long. The Spirit descended upon them, giving them the ability to speak in many languages, empowering them to share the good news. Into the streets they went, to tell everyone what they had witnessed. With passion and skill they told all they encountered about Jesus. They were so enthusiastic that some who saw them assumed that they must be drunk, for in their experience nothing else could explain such behavior.

The church—empowered by the Spirit—is to be a community of passion committed to sharing about Jesus.

A question to consider: would anyone ever think members of our congregation were drunk because of their passion for Jesus?

Acts 2:43–47. The fervent faith of those early days was a great attractor. Even in the seeming chaos brought on by the unleashing of the Spirit, faith in Jesus drew more and more people into the fellowship. Men and women joined the once small group by the thousands. What had been *a* small group became *many* small groups that continued to meet together in homes to pray, to learn from the apostles, and to break bread. And they shared with each other. They, as Acts puts it, "had all things in common" (2:44). What is being described here, beyond the pooling of monetary resources, is a depth of sharing with each other that can only be described as devotion to each other.

The church is to be a community of deep devotion, not only to Jesus, but also to each other—a devotion demonstrated in a depth of sharing.

A question to consider: is our congregation one in which there is an intimacy of sharing?

Acts 3:1–10. The pattern of those early days in Jerusalem was to spend time together in small groups in homes and also to worship at the temple. It is while they were on their way to worship that Peter and John were starkly confronted with the needs of the world in the form of a disabled man, begging for the money he needed to sustain his life. Peter asked the man to look at him, establishing a personal connection. He clearly stated what he couldn't do, which was to fall into the pattern of everyone else who wanted to help him. He then offered the unique gift he did have—a gift far greater than silver or gold, the power of Jesus to bring healing.

The church is to be a community that understands that what it offers to the world is unique because of the power of Jesus at work in and through its members.

A question to consider: are we clear about what we cannot offer others even though they ask for it and what, in the name of Jesus Christ, we do have to offer?

Acts 4:23–31. Peter was quick to explain the power that enabled him to heal the man: it was the same power that raised Jesus from the dead, the same Jesus they had crucified. Talk like this was bound to lead to trouble and it did. Peter and John were put in jail for the night and then brought before the authorities. Although the Jewish leaders were troubled by their talk, the support of the people for these men who had the power to heal forced them to release Peter and John with only a stern warning. After this intense interaction with both the suffering and injustice of the world, the two disciples returned to the community of believers to share their experience and to pray. And what did they pray for? Not protection, not for a change of heart in those who wanted to persecute them, not even for strength to face their ordeal. Together the community prayed for boldness so that they might continue to share the good news—boldness so that they wouldn't be afraid to get into trouble again!

The church is to be a community that trusts in the power of the Holy Spirit to enable it to live boldly in order to participate in God's mission in the world.

A question to consider: in the face of opposition and imprisonment for our faith, would it be boldness for which we prayed?

Acts 5:1–11. The church's commitment to sharing provides the backdrop for this incident. Ananius and Sapphira sold their property to give the proceeds to the community but held back a portion of it for themselves. Peter, who clearly had not taken a course in pastoral counseling, confronted the husband with his deception and he immediately dropped dead. When the wife arrived shortly thereafter, the pattern was repeated: Peter confronted her with the deception and she dropped dead. This passage undoubtedly causes us some measure of discomfort. It is not, after all, what we want to experience when we go to church on Sunday. There is, however, much to be learned from it. What is most striking is that this is where Luke first uses the world "church" in Acts. Could it be that something happened here that is central to the identity of the church? If so, that something is related to the deception that took place, the inability of those involved to be honest with others in the community and with God. That is the sin that Peter confronts, for honesty with each other and before God is absolutely necessary to the existence of the church. The life of disciples is not only a matter of belief; it is also about the way we live. It is essential that within the community, disciples are held accountable for the faithfulness of their actions. It's what makes a church a church.

The church is to be a community of truth in which there is accountability as its members seek to live as faithful disciples.

A question to consider: are we willing to take the risk of being truth-tellers and holding others accountable for their actions as followers of Jesus?

Acts 6:1–7. The astonishing growth of the church brought new problems. The apostles were overwhelmed by the demands that were placed upon them and as a result an important part of their ministry was suffering. Some of the widows were not getting their fair share of the daily food distribution. The solution was to appoint additional people to fill this role so that the apostles could attend to the preaching of the word. This wasn't an issue of ministry versus maintenance. It wasn't even an issue of the relative importance of the tasks. Both the distribution and the preaching were ministry. Both were essential aspects of the church's mission. Neither could be neglected. This was a practical problem that needed to be resolved. It wasn't a matter of affixing blame, but of enhancing ministry. The apostles, because of their participation in the ministry of Jesus, were uniquely qualified for the ministry of preaching. Others, if they were "of good standing, full of the Spirit and of wisdom" (Acts 6:3), had the gifts needed for the care of those in the community. To resolve this practical problem of how best to carry out its mission, the church changed its organizational structure, tasks were reassigned, new leaders were selected, and the mission was carried out more effectively.

The church is to be a community in which mission determines both leadership positions and those who fill them.

A question to consider: is our effective engagement in mission the main reason for the roles and structures of our congregation?

Acts 7:54–60. The tensions that began with the imprisonment of Peter reached their climax in the stoning of Stephen. He was one of those selected to fill the new role in the church. Clearly his faith mattered to him—more than life itself. His great crime, it seems, was that he saw things differently than most people and he wasn't afraid to talk about it. So when he recited the history of Israel from his perspective as a Christian the people were incensed. Their frenzy intensified as he claimed to see Jesus himself standing on the right hand of God. And so, he was dragged from the city and stoned. It may seem like a useless death. We might think it could have been avoided if Stephen had been more politically astute or if he'd had training in conflict resolution. We may think it has little to do with today's better mannered society. But there is something about the starkness of this passage that doesn't let us escape so easily. Stephen believed enough in Jesus, in who he was and what he taught, to die for him.

The church is to be a community that sees things differently because of Jesus and lives according to the way it sees.

A question to consider: do we have the courage of our teachings?

Acts 8:1–5. The stoning of Stephen led to a more general persecution of Christians in Jerusalem. Except for the apostles, most believers scattered to other cities or to a life of constant travel. But they could not keep quiet. Despite what had happened to Stephen, despite the clear danger involved in speaking as he did, they continued to talk about Jesus and what his life, death, and resurrection meant for everyone. Philip went to Samaria. Persecution and suffering were the reasons for the movement of the early Christians out of Jerusalem and the fulfillment of Christ's prophecy that his disciples would be his witnesses "in Jerusalem. . . in Samaria . . ." (Acts 1:8). It was, to be sure, the strength of these early disciples' convictions that turned this would-be tragedy into a glorious new chapter in the spread of the gospel. But more than that, it is testimony to the power of the Holy Spirit at work in the community of faith. When difficulties emerge, when tension and stress prevail, when old ways of being and doing are no longer possible, new opportunities emerge and have the potential to lead faithful disciples into new arenas of ministry—if the Spirit is present.

The church is to be a community that never ceases to attend to its mission.

A question to consider: do we use the difficulties and trials we face as new opportunities to witness?

Acts 8:9–25. The community of the early church faced challenges to its purpose and integrity both from without and within. The fate of Ananius and Sapphira didn't forever eliminate the temptation money provided. As the church expanded to new places this same challenge was encountered again and again. In Samaria, Simon, a magician of note, heard Philip preach and believed. Following his baptism he spent much time with Philip, amazed at all he was able to do. What really impressed him, however, was the gift of the Holy Spirit that Peter was able to bestow. Being a practical sort of guy he went to Peter and asked how much it would cost for him to be given this ability to give the Holy Spirit to others. Peter was enraged. Today's English Version translates his response more bluntly than most: "May you and your money go to hell, for thinking that you can buy God's gift with money!" (Acts 8:20, TEV). Remember, Simon is not some unbelieving infidel. He is a believer who has been baptized and is a member of the community of faith in Samaria. He has even gone out of his way to spend time with Philip in order to learn more about his new faith. There is no evidence that his profession of faith was not genuine or even that he was seeking personal advantage. Despite his faith, despite his baptism, despite the time spent with Philip he still didn't grasp the fullness of what it meant to be a follower of Jesus. (He sounds a bit like the original disciples in that, doesn't he?) He remained confused about the role that money plays in faith and in the life of the community. He believed that his access to financial resources should put him in a privileged position to exercise the prerogatives of the faith. He was wrong! And Peter made the error of his ways clear to him. He then called on Simon to repent and ask God's forgiveness for thinking such a thing.

The church is to be a community that rejects the world's currency for God's economy of grace.

A question to consider: is money our prerequisite for mission or do we believe that the power of the Spirit is sufficient?

Acts 8:26–40. After this episode with Simon, Philip was probably seeking some rest. But it was not to be. No less than an angel came to him and told him to get himself down to the desert road between Jerusalem and Gaza in the middle of the day. This was neither a comfortable nor reasonable place to be, because no one would travel along a desert road in the middle of the day. But, clearly the angel knew more than Philip, for on that road Philip encountered a chariot containing an official of the Ethiopian queen's court on his way home after a visit to Jerusalem. While probably not a Jew, he was a religious man who had been in Jerusalem to worship. As he rode along he was reading from the prophet Isaiah. When Philip joined him in the chariot he began to ask questions, which Philip answered, explaining that Jesus was the fulfillment of the promise he was reading. Struck by the truth and power of Philip's testimony, the Ethiopian stopped the chariot and asked to be baptized. When he emerged from the water after baptism Philip disappeared and the Ethiopian continued on his way filled with joy.

The church is to be a community that sends its members into places where they will encounter those for whom the gospel can make a difference.

A question to consider: are we willing to listen to the Spirit and go where the Spirit tells us to go in order to share the gospel, even if it seems ludicrous?

Acts 15:1–21. As the church grew it became more diverse. Most importantly both Jews and Gentiles became members. So, for this new faith that had its foundations in Judaism the question became: how Jewish do you need to be in order to be a Christian? There were those who believed that adherence to the Jewish law was essential for everyone who was a Christian. There were others who believed that the ritual practices of Judaism were no longer essential. In the manner of all churches they had a meeting to resolve the controversy. There was intense debate; there was heated discussion. But this meeting ended in a resolution everyone could live with. Gentile Christians need not be circumcised, but they did need to observe four practices that were required of all those who lived in Israel, whether Jew or Gentile. This wasn't the final resolution of the issue, but it was one the church could live with; it was one that allowed it to continue to focus on mission rather than debate what personal practices entitled or disqualified one from being a Christian.

The church is to be a community of diverse opinions and practices based in a common devotion to Jesus and a shared commitment to his mission.

A question to consider: are we willing to talk together about our different opinions and practices in order to discover new ways of being faithful to our mission?

Acts 19:21–41. The church, even this small and upstart church, exists in the world. It cannot separate itself from the world; it cannot avoid the social and economic implications of its beliefs and practices. Nowhere is that clash more apparent than in Paul's experience in Ephesus. The conversion of so many former devotees of the goddess Artemis created a crisis in town. These new Christians no longer believed that silver artisans could craft gods. The silversmith trade was in jeopardy. But the problem was greater than that, for Artemis played a special role in the life of Ephesus. Her major temple was here. She was a virgin goddess and defender of chastity. The religion surrounding her touched every aspect of the life of Ephesus. "It was a civil religion, and the rhythm of city life revolved around the temple and its festivals. To subvert the worship of Artemis the Great was to threaten the city's culture—its way of life, both economic and social—shaped by its routines and calendar."[6] By preaching about Jesus and winning believers Paul had made himself a threat to all of this. The people of the city, led by the silversmiths, simply would not stand for it. A near riot ensued, until the city clerk was able to quiet the crowd and Paul could go on his way. An Anglican bishop is reported to have said, "Wherever Paul went they had riots. Wherever I go they serve tea." What does that say about the present power of the church to transform the lives of people according to the teachings of Jesus?

The church is to be a community that supports its members as they translate the teachings of Jesus into concrete ways of living in the world.

A question to consider: are we willing to challenge the social and economic practices of the world in order to remain faithful to Jesus?

Acts 28:23–31. The story of Acts ends in Rome. Paul was there, following a perilous journey, to stand trial as a Roman citizen on charges brought by those in Jerusalem. Upon his arrival he contacted the Jews of Rome to meet with them to talk about his arrest, but even more about the Messiah they were seeking. As was always the case, some believed and some did not. But Paul was undaunted. Under arrest, facing almost certain execution, he continued to preach, continued to remain convinced that salvation was at hand for all those who would listen and believe. It was this faith and confidence that enabled him, even under these conditions, to continue his work "with all boldness and without hindrance" (Acts 28:31).

The church is to be a community that lives and dies in the faith that God's mission will be fulfilled.

A question to consider: do we have absolute confidence in the power of God's Word to reach, touch, and transform everyone?

❖❖❖

In exploring the ministry of Jesus and of the early church we have been able to describe key elements of the "basics" of purpose and mission of the church. We've learned that forming disciples of Jesus Christ is basic to the identity of the church. Before we move on, however, we need to look at the mandate that was given to the disciples and through them to the church by Jesus. His parting words to them have, from the very beginning, been looked upon as the foundation of Christian mission. It is to those words that we now turn.

THE GREAT COMMISSION

Go therefore and make disciples of all nations;
baptizing them in the name of the Father and of the Son and of the
    Holy Spirit,
and teaching them to obey everything that I have commanded you.
And remember, I am with you always, to the end of the age.

These are Jesus' final words to the disciples in Matthew 28:19–20. They appear in other forms in other Gospels, but Matthew's account has captured the imagination of many with its seeming command to go into the world.[7] There's no better place to begin when we're trying to get back to the basics of what we're here for than this passage. We're not interested in doing a sophisticated linguistic study here, but there are points of this translation that have significant impact on our understanding of the commission that Jesus gave his followers.

A direct translation of the Greek in this passage would go something like this:

Going therefore disciple you all the nations,
    baptizing them in the name of the Father and of the Son and of the
        Holy Spirit,

teaching them to observe all things whatever I gave command to you;
and behold I with you am all the days until the completion of the
age.[8]

The most striking feature of this literal translation in the "ing"
form of going, baptizing, and teaching. This contrasts with the usual
translation, in which only baptizing and teaching appear in this
form. In the Greek the main verb is disciple, not *make* disciples.
"Go" is not an imperative, as is disciple.[9] The usual translation ("Go
. . . and make disciples. . .) makes it seem as though both "go" and
"make disciples" carry equal weight in the passage or even that
"go" is the primary verb. As a result, this passage is often used,
stressing "go," as a mandate for evangelism. The inclusion of the
word "make" in the translation, rather than leaving it simply as
disciple, has compounded the tendency to see this passage as a
mandate for evangelism, because it leads fairly naturally to an assumption that the task is to turn nondisciples (heathens, the unchurched) into followers of Christ. While evangelism certainly isn't
alien to the spirit of the passage, its mandate is not evangelism, but
discipleship. The verb is disciple. The commission is to disciple.

A second important element of the translation is the use of the
word "nations." While the direct translation quoted earlier uses
this term, the Greek word is more typically translated as Gentiles.
It is not nations that are to be discipled, but people.[10] This, of course,
makes sense in that discipling a political entity is not possible. Only
people can be discipled; only people can be disciples.

When these insights are taken into consideration, a translation
of the Great Commission that better captures its intent might be:

As you are going into the world, disciple all people,
baptizing them in the name of the Father and of the Son and of the
   Holy Spirit,
and teaching them to obey everything that I have commanded you.
And, I am with you to the end of the age.

The assumption is that disciples are going into the world; that
is where they live out their lives, after all. The commission is to
disciple all people as they are living their lives in the world.

It should be noted as well that this commission is to the eleven disciples as a group (and through them to the church). Although the disciples will carry out the commission to disciple others, the commission itself is given to the group. It is the church as a community of disciples that is now the custodian of the commission. The commission given to the church is to be a community that makes/shapes/grows/nurtures/teaches/forms disciples.

We, as Christ's disciples in the church, have been given a commission. We are to be disciples and together in the community of faith we are to form disciples. When we go back to the basics that is what we discover. Our look at the ministry of Jesus helped us learn more about what a disciple is. Our look at the mission of the church in Acts helped us learn more about the role of the church in forming disciples. Now it's time to see what all of this means for us in our time and place.

Three ❖ The Life of the Disciple

I HAVE A FRIEND. HE'S BEEN DESCRIBED BY THOSE WHO know him as an "odd combination of Midwestern ideals and Far Eastern feng shui." He grew up in Ohio. His family was marginally religious—belonging to a church, attending every now and then. In his adolescence he experimented with various forms of risky behavior—nothing terrible, but not what parents would want their son to do. When he graduated from college he went off to Hong Kong for four years to work. While there he was on a basketball team that played some games against a traveling team of Christians from the United States. There was something about the quality of their lives and the reality of their relationship with Christ that captivated him and led to a desire to grow in his own relationship with Christ. When he returned to the United States for a new job, he got an apartment and joined a nearby church, assuming this would be a place his relationship with Christ would be nurtured in a way that would impact his life. They put him on a committee.

This experience provides a snapshot of the clash of cultures that is taking place in American religious life today. A church whose identity and function were shaped by one world is finding it increasingly difficult to remain relevant in the new world that is now emerging. It struggles to understand a faithfulness that incorporates both American ideals and Far Eastern feng shui. It fails to come to terms with involvement that isn't based in joining, with participation that refuses to hold office. It misses the deep spiritual yearning of countless people of all ages as it continues its increasingly futile attempts to maintain an outmoded organizational structure. It simply doesn't recognize the power of Christ to attract, transform, and empower. It is afraid to let that power loose in its own life and through it into the community. When confronted by a person who is seeking to grow in relationship with Christ, all it knows to do is put that person on a committee.

But what if this church were to rediscover its purpose as a disciple-forming community? What if it ordered its life in such a way that everything it did helped people grow in their relationship with Christ and live out the reality of that relationship in all their relationships? That is the challenge that confronts us on our journey.

The Bible makes it pretty clear. We are to disciple all people. We are to do that through our engagement with the world; we are to do that by baptizing and teaching; we are to do that in the confidence that Christ is with us in this work.

Before we plunge into a discussion of how we fulfill this great commission, however, it will be helpful to think a bit about what all these things mean—especially since the world in which we are currently engaged is so different from the one in which the church existed for so long.

Who is a Disciple?

Let's think first of all about this word *disciple*. What is a disciple anyway? Two words that are particularly important for our understanding are *learner* and *follower*. A disciple is a learner—he or she wants to learn more about the teachings and way of life of a particular person. Something about that person has attracted the disciple. A curiosity has been sparked that needs to be satisfied. So the disciple wants to learn. But this learning isn't just a head trip. It's not simply an intellectual exercise that can be done in the confines of a study or library. The disciple wants to do more than learn; the disciple also wants to follow. That is really what the learning is all about. A disciple learns so he or she can follow. And it is through following that the disciple learns. The curiosity about the person is more than idle; it's active. The attraction is about lifestyle and being. The disciple, as much as possible, wants to emulate the person. So, a beginning point in describing a Christian disciple would be to say that this person is someone who desires to learn more about Jesus so he or she can follow Jesus more fully.

I grew up in the faith. I went to Sunday school regularly as a child and learned about the Bible. By the time I reached junior high school I knew the Bible pretty well and I also knew what Baptists believed about God, Jesus, sin, and all the other basic beliefs of Christianity. That didn't make me a disciple, however. At some point in this process I became intrigued by this man Jesus. His teaching spoke to me. His care and concern for others inspired me. His willingness to die for faith challenged me. The assurance of salvation that his death offered changed me. At some point in the process of learning about Jesus I became so intrigued that I decided I wanted to be more like this person myself. It was that decision that led to my baptism. I didn't know as much about Jesus then as I know now. I didn't know as much about what it means to follow Jesus then as I know now. But I knew enough—enough to want to learn more so that I could follow. I became a disciple.

There is more to it than that, however. Our brief look at the Gospels and Acts made it pretty clear that no one ever really makes it to complete "disciplehood." Even those who were with Jesus every day for several years still struggled to understand what following Jesus was all about. And they got it wrong a good bit of the time! Even after they set out on their own after Jesus' ascension they still kept learning more about what it meant to be a disciple. As they confronted new situations and new issues they had to work out what it meant to follow Jesus. It was the same for me. It's the same for all of us. We never arrive; we are always in process. So a disciple is engaged in a lifelong process of learning how to follow, learning what it means to live as a follower of Jesus. It doesn't stop when formal children's and youth Sunday school classes end. It isn't over at baptism or confirmation. It can't be confined to a limited period of time after a person becomes a Christian. We never reach an age at which we can say we have learned all we need to know about following Jesus. It is one of the great challenges of faith that will only be completed in eternity.

It would help to explore the notion of "following" a bit at this point, because Christians have a particularly interesting perspective on this. We believe that following Jesus is what life is really all about. In a very real sense, God put us on this earth so that we can follow Jesus. It all has to do with God's plan for creation. A lot has been written about this and it can lead us into some pretty heavy theology, but the essence of it is this: God wants to bring all creation back in line with God's original intention that it be good—fully, totally, completely good. The way this often gets talked about is to say that God wants to redeem all creation. God's purpose in sending Jesus into the world was to accomplish this task—to redeem all creation. The Letter to the Ephesians puts it this way: "With all wisdom and insight he has made known to us the mystery of his will, according to his good pleasure that he set forth in Christ, as a plan for the fullness of time, to gather up all things in him, things in heaven and things on earth" (Ephesians 1:8–10). When all things are gathered up in God, all creation will be redeemed. This was the purpose of Christ's ministry, death, and resurrection. So, as followers of Jesus our purpose is also to be involved in the redemption of all creation. It sounds pretty fantastic, doesn't it? What I do, the way I choose to live my life, makes a difference in God's plan to redeem all creation! It's a bit overwhelming. In fact, it sounds so overwhelming it could lead us to give up before we begin. The challenge seems just too great.

If we were left to our own devices the challenge would be too great. We would fail miserably. But God hasn't left us on our own. We'll keep coming back to this to look at different ways in which God provides for us in this work so that we are not left to ourselves, but for now we can just repeat the affirmation that this is why God put us on earth in the first place. The truth Christians live by is that God has intentions for us and for the way in which we will participate in this great challenge. We discover those intentions as we discover our own particular call from God.

That word "call" has a long history within Christian thinking. It has been used largely to talk about "full time Christian ministry" and the way clergy determine if this is the right direction for their lives. But it's not just for clergy; it's for everyone who wants to be a disciple. The way in which each one of us is to live as a disciple depends upon God's call to us—God's intention for the role we should play in the mission of redeeming all creation.

This isn't just an esoteric theological concept, however. It relates directly to issues we deal with regularly throughout our lives. The half-jesting comments about deciding what we will do with the rest of our lives or when we "grow up" are common ways of expressing a concern about call. When we think about the job we want to have, when we consider whether or not we will get married or have children, when we make any decisions about what we will be and do in our lives, we are dealing with this issue of call. The unique perspective the disciple brings to answering these questions is the understanding that the best answer depends upon the way God wants us to be involved in the great mission of redeeming all creation.

Disciples don't just materialize, however. Becoming and growing as a disciple is a process. That process is called discipleship. From our discussion so far, we can now offer a description of discipleship as: the ongoing, lifelong process of discerning and living out God's call to be the person God created you to be as you participate in God's purpose in creation in your particular time and place.

Affirmations about Discipleship

Before we move on to consider what it takes for us to grow as disciples, let's pause to make a few affirmations about this process of discipleship.

Discipleship is for all God's people. God doesn't play favorites. All of us are created for a particular purpose; God is calling each one of us to live as a disciple. There are no distinctions of rank, no in-crowd and out-crowd. There isn't a special or better discipleship for clergy over laity or men over women or adults over youth. The

concept of the priesthood of all believers is central to our understanding of discipleship. This belief acknowledges that each one of
us stands directly before God with no need for intermediaries. Each
of us receives God's blessings and each of us is directly accountable
to God for our life and faith. In our priesthood we are called to
ministry in the world, acting as God's agents. Discipleship is for all
God's people in another sense, as well. The work of disciples is for
the benefit of all God's people, as it is work that is part of God's
mission of redemption of all creation. That's discipleship.

Discipleship depends upon our response. God's call to discipleship
comes to everyone. It is our response, however, that determines
whether or not we will be disciples. It's a matter of how we choose
to live our lives, how we understand our purpose. If a desire for
power or affluence governs the decisions we make about how we
will live our lives, it's quite likely we will not be living as the people
God created us to be. If, on the other hand, we choose to approach
life's decisions from the perspective of God's call and involvement
in God's mission, we are disciples—even though at times we may
fail to live out our disciplehood as God intends. Part if it is a matter
of perspective—how we choose to look at life concerns and decisions. Do we see them exclusively from a business or financial or
psychological perspective, or do we see them primarily as faith issues? This, of course, isn't to say that we cannot draw on the insights that a business or financial or psychological perspective might
bring. The key, however, is that a faith perspective shapes and governs our decision-making. Part of it is perspective; the other part is
performance—what we actually do. Hopefully our perspective
shapes our actions so that they follow naturally from the choices
we have made about what we believe. The faith perspective leads
us to make decisions that result in actions that enable us to live
more fully as disciples. Discipleship involves both what we believe
and how we live. Our response comes in both thought and action.
It's the response that makes us disciples.

Discipleship happens within the community of faith. There is no
such thing as a solitary disciple. At times we may be alone, but we
are never solitary. One-to-one relationships may be important in
discipleship, but they cannot carry the full load. Important discipleship experiences may occur outside the bounds of congrega-

tional life, but disciples always come from and return to the community. The community of faith is essential to forming disciples. The community is the bearer of the tradition—the Story that tells of God's purpose, the salvation of Christ's sacrifice, the Spirit at work in and among us to attune us to God's presence and power. The community provides the setting in which our call can be discerned. Only the community brings together the variety of gifts and experiences that are essential for discipleship. It takes a community to form a disciple.

ELEMENTS OF DISCIPLESHIP

Now we come to the very practical issue of how this all happens. What needs to be part of the life of a person in order to grow as a disciple? There are probably as many ways to answer this question as there are disciples, for we are all unique persons who relate and learn and minister in unique ways. Recognizing that uniqueness, we can still provide a framework that honors it yet provides a basic sense of direction for all disciples. I'll introduce that framework here so that we will have a general overview of it. In the next chapter I'll talk more about it and what it means for churches.

In order for a person to grow as a disciple of Jesus Christ regular experiences of deepening, equipping, and ministering are essential.[1]

Deepening is about relationships—with God, self, and others. The foundational relationship of the disciple is with God in Jesus Christ. It is that relationship that has touched and transformed the person, that relationship that has led the person to stake a life claim on being a disciple. Discipleship is a continuing process of growth in relationship with God as Creator, Christ, and Spirit—experiencing in ever-deepening ways the fullness of God. The relationship with one's self is also a growing relationship for the disciple. The inward journey is important because it enables us to know ourselves well enough to understand how God is at work in us and what God seeks from us. The personal growth this inward journey brings is essential because it is in this growth that we set aside the old self and become more able to serve others in Christ's name.

The third dimension of deepening is growth in relationship with others in community. The disciple depends upon the community of faith. Ideally that community will be the local congregation, but this doesn't always happen. At times the disciple will need to seek his or her community of faith in other places, among those who share the commitments of being a disciple and with whom the person is able to develop relationships of depth, integrity, and truth. Without this kind of community, the disciple cannot live.

Equipping is about preparation. It has two dimensions: gifts/ call and skills/knowledge. We've already looked at the importance of call for the disciple. That call is, among other things, based in the gifts God has given us. Part of our uniqueness rests in these gifts, which have been part of us since we were born. They are what shape our personality and abilities. Recognizing these gifts is important to the disciple, because they are the means through which we participate in God's mission in the world. That is, they are what we bring to the mix. So knowing and nurturing gifts, which leads to a sense of call, is the first dimension of equipping. The second dimension is skills and knowledge. Disciples need to know certain things and be able to do certain things. Some of these are for all disciples. All of us, for example, need to know about the Bible and how to use it in our lives and faith. Other skills and knowledge are specific. They are determined by call. The skills and knowledge we need will differ, for example, if our call is to work with at-risk youth, provide leadership in a business, be a teacher, or serve as clergy.

Ministering is about involvement. It is our participation in God's mission of redeeming all creation. The gifts we have, the call we receive, the skills and knowledge we acquire are put to the test in ministering. This can happen both within and outside the church. Leaders and teachers are needed within the community of faith. That may be the call of some. For most disciples, however, ministering will occur outside the church, through their various involvements in the world.

❖

Deepening, equipping, and ministering are the three essential elements in the life of a disciple. Ongoing experiences in each of these three areas are what make disciples and nurture their continuing growth.

We should also note at this point what these elements are not. They are not three steps in a "discipling" process. It is not a matter of getting "deepened" and "equipped" so that we can then go out and "minister." All three are present at all times in the life of the disciple. All three continually contribute to the growth of the disciple and all three are constantly playing off each other. It is only as all three elements are taken together and inform each other that we continue to grow as disciples.

Before we move on to explore each of these elements in more detail let's take a moment to admit the limitations of this pursuit. We have been very analytical in this discussion. We've defined three elements of discipleship, three kinds of experiences that disciples need to have in order to continue to grow. Everything is neat and clean. This is good because it helps us gain some clarity about what is going on in our own lives and what we need to be about in order to discover the new answers to what it means to be a church in today's world. But in doing this we run the risk of making it too antiseptic, too neat and clean. We run the risk of creating little boxes into which we then try to cram our faith experiences. Life and faith are never that neat. There is always a messiness to them. In my own life being a disciple never works the way I have just described it. Certainly I can recognize experiences of deepening, equipping, and ministering. But many of them were haphazard. Many others I didn't recognize until they had come and gone. Some of them I didn't even recognize as faith experiences at all until much later.

What was one of the most significant conversion experiences in my life occurred this way. I was having a conversation with a friend. It was at a critical point in my life, as I was trying to break out of some old patterns of behavior. I poured out my struggle to him, describing what seemed to me to be an inevitable pattern of wallowing in doubts about myself and why I did the things I did. As a way to describe my plight I said something like this: "I worry about why I have done something and then worry about why I am worrying about it and then worry about why I am worrying about why I am worrying about it." He looked me straight in the eye and said, "That's the stupidest thing I've ever heard." And in that moment I suddenly knew he was right. The bluntness of his words shocked me into the realization that I was caught in a pattern of behavior that made it impossible for me to become more than I was. I saw for the first time that it really was a "stupid" thing I was doing. Even more importantly, I realized that I could change this if I really wanted to do so. It was a new beginning point for me.

This experience was not explicitly religious. And yet I now see it as one of the most profound deepening experiences of my life. The first way in which this became apparent was as an experience of deepening relationship with myself—I came to know myself better because of it and in that new knowledge was able to move into a new way of being. Then I came to see it as an experience of deepening relationship with others. Because of the comment of this one friend I came to see the importance of community in ways I had not seen it before. It is the community that provides the setting in which truth—even difficult truth—can be told. Without that experience I would not have been able to break out of my old ways of being. Through it I developed a new willingness to risk the vulnerability that is essential to community, because I had a powerful experience of the transformation that community makes possible. Finally, I came to understand the experience as one of deepening relationship with God. This took a bit longer because it was less obvious. But over time I came to understand that God was at work in all of this. It was God's Spirit that led me to speak honestly and enabled my friend to respond with even greater honesty. It was God's Spirit that provided the community in which truth could be spoken. And, ultimately, it was the grace of God that brought me to a new way of being. There is for me no other way to explain what was going on in that experience. Through it, as I have gone deeper in relationship with myself and with others, God became more real for me. No longer just a concept, God became a powerful, transforming, life-giving presence.

And so, even though we will be analytical, even though we will define and describe abstract concepts, let's always remember what we say is not the reality. What we say is only our inevitably feeble attempt to describe the wondrous workings of God on us and in us and through us as we seek to become more the people God created us to be.

Four ❖ The Elements of Discipleship

W━━HEN I WAS GROWING UP THERE WAS AN EMPTY LOT at the end of a street not far from our home. It was pretty overgrown—weeds, shrubs, trees, and dead limbs everywhere. But once every year a group of people would gather on that lot to say a few prayers and sing a few hymns. It seems the lot was owned by a religious society (a family chapel, really), and the requirement of the deed was that they hold religious services there in order to retain their tax-exempt status. A few prayers, a few hymns once a year and the requirement could be satisfied. I wonder how much like this "religious society" many churches actually are. They go through the motions to satisfy the requirements, but are they really churches—at least in the way God intends churches to be churches? They may perform good deeds in the community, but so do service organizations. They may provide fellowship, but so do fraternal organizations. They may help people get a better handle on their lives, but so do self-help and recovery groups. They may use all the right kind of pious language. They may have worship and Sunday school and Vacation Bible School and all the right kinds of boards and committees. But the only question that matters is: do they offer to people, both members and others, real opportunities to experience the transforming love of Christ in ways that touch their greatest needs, heal their deepest hurts, and fulfill their highest hopes—in ways that, to put it a bit differently, lead them to be the people God created them to be?

I believe that the key to congregations being able to lead people to become the people God created them to be lies in the recovery of the church's identity as a disciple-forming community.

I believe that when a congregation begins to live out this understanding of itself it will move beyond the worry and malaise that are so evident today and into a new day of being a transformative presence in the lives of people and communities.

I believe this new day will be extremely challenging and sometimes very chaotic, but this will be a sign of the Spirit's presence and power at work.

I believe that the alternative to this challenge and chaos is death.

The empty lot is now a Burger King.

The brief overview of discipleship in the previous chapter offers us a beginning point for this new way of being for the congregation. Remember its basic assumptions:

- God created each one of us for a particular purpose.
- That purpose is related to participation in God's mission of redeeming all creation.
- We find our role in that mission by answering God's call to become disciples of Jesus Christ.
- It is in living as disciples that we find our true vocation and meaning in life.
- The essential experiences of discipleship, for finding our true vocation and meaning, are those that provide opportunities for deepening, equipping, and ministering.

Our aim in this chapter will be to explore the three elements of discipleship more thoroughly. As we do that it will be important to keep two perspectives in mind. First, there is the personal perspective. If we are to become and continue to grow as disciples, deepening, equipping, and ministering will need to be part of our lives on a continuing basis. The question for each one of us is: in what ways am I participating in experiences of deepening, equipping, and ministering? Secondly, there is the congregational perspective. If persons need experiences of deepening, equipping, and ministering to become and grow as disciples, one way to understand the role of the congregation is as a provider of these experiences. It is through providing experiences of deepening, equipping, and ministering that the congregation becomes a disciple-forming community. The question for the congregation is: in what ways does our congregation provide experiences of deepening, equipping and ministering?

DEEPENING—GROWING IN RELATIONSHIP

Deepening is about relationships—with God, with self, with others in community. As growth happens in one of these it is enhanced in the others; they are intricately related to each other.

To be a disciple of Jesus Christ means, first and foremost, to have a relationship with him. That relationship can begin at any point in life. For some, such as myself, it exists even before conscious memory, starting in the arms of a mother and father of faith and in a Sunday school nursery. For others it comes later, perhaps with dramatic suddenness in the midst of a crisis or some great turning point in life. For all of us, however, no matter when we date the beginning of the relationship, Christ has always been there, eager to be in relationship, ready to begin. Christ is there, seeking, because this is one dimension of God's mission of redeeming all creation—the redeeming of each person. The disciple is one who has responded to this seeking presence by saying yes to relationship with Jesus. For the faithful disciple this relationship continues to grow. Like any relationship, it has its ebbs and flows, times of excitement and calm, times of intensity and dullness. Like any relationship, when it is not attended to it withers, when it becomes stagnant it dies, when it is taken for granted it becomes shallow. Faithful disciples attend to their relationship with Christ so that it will continue to deepen, to become richer, and to shape their identity as persons.

The disciple-forming community supports this growing relationship in its life and ministry. It does that first and foremost in worship that encourages the experience of the holy and brings participants into a sense of God's presence and power. It does it also as it encourages the practice of spiritual disciplines. We need to do more than wish for a deeper relationship with God. We need to engage in actions that allow that relationship to grow. The disciple-forming congregation is a repository of spiritual disciplines; it is familiar with the disciplines that have aided disciples across the ages to grow in their relationship with Christ, and it provides the setting in which these disciplines can be tested and adapted.

The disciplines are both individual and corporate—to be part of both the personal and community life of the disciple. Richard Foster's classic, *Celebration of Discipline,* provides insight into the "inward" disciplines of meditation, prayer, fasting, and study; the "outward" disciplines of simplicity, solitude, submission, and service; and the corporate disciplines of confession, worship, guidance, and celebration.[1] It is important to remember that while all of these are spiritual disciplines that enhance our deepening relationship with God, they can also play a significant role in equipping and ministering.

Not every discipline will work for every person. Some will need more reflective experiences, others more active; some more study-oriented, others more prayerful. At its most effective, however, this concern for growing in relationship with Christ infuses every aspect of the disciple-forming congregation. It is apparent in the work of boards, in the Sunday school, and on the mission field.

Deepening also includes growth in relationship with self. This dimension comes both as a way to and as a result of our deepening relationship with God. As long ago as the desert fathers and mothers in the fourth century it was recognized that increased self-knowledge was one means of growing in relationship with God.[2] The basis of their spiritual discipline was that as we go deeper into ourselves we go deeper into our relationship with God. That is what I learned through the experience I described at the end of the previous chapter.

And yet, the reverse is also true. For as our relationship with God deepens, as we experience God's love, forgiveness, and grace more fully, as we trust in these more completely, our ability to go more deeply into ourselves grows. Our confidence in God's love and grace allows us to face our sin and our real self because we know more fully that "If we confess our sins, he who is faithful and just will forgive us our sins and cleanse us from all unrighteousness" (1 John 1:9). This knowledge gives us the freedom to go deep into ourselves.

Carlyle Marney wrote about the feathers that we put on to cover us up and protect us, feathers that keep us from being the people God intends us to be. He believed there was no hope for us as Christians unless we started to molt! He wrote:

> There is no redemption and any claim to salvation is a farce unless it penetrates sooner or later all these treasured feathers of our views of the self—and—this hurts! This hurts because our feathers have grown to us. Yet this is the truth I shout from the housetops: There is no growth that is Christian without the nerve to submit to the correcting of my images of the self. I now see it clearly: the spinal cord of redemption is the nerve to submit all my images of the self to the Christ and his people for correction. This is Christian fulfillment, Christian growth, and it is superbly Christian education of adults the hard way; and the Book is clear, if you wish a text: "If any would come after me let him deny himself. . ."[3]

This is how I understand the reality of original sin in my own life. It is the struggle, so great that at times it seems to be my inability to submit myself to Christ in this way. My fear is too great, which (if I am honest with myself) is another way of saying my faith is too small. And yet, this is in a real sense what it is all about. This is the essence of what God wants for us and why Christ died for us. It is so we can become new beings, setting aside the sin or whatever name you put to it that keeps us from being what God created us to be. That's a very personal thing, but it is also a corporate thing, because from a Christian perspective you can't have one without the other. This dynamic works itself into everything we are about—from our personal lives to our families to our own ministries to our ability to ask the questions that are essential to our continued faithfulness as a people. In the face of such original sin what can we do except continue to try to gather the faith that enables us to submit—and, of course, continue to give thanks for the mystery of God's grace!

This is how a deepening relationship with Christ and a deepening relationship with self are connected. To relate deeply to Christ as a disciple can be seen as a process of submitting to Christ. It is also possible to view it as the nurturing and development of the "Christ in you" that Paul speaks about in Colossians 1:17. From both perspectives, however, knowing ourselves deeply is essential, so that we can differentiate between what is Christ and what are our own foibles and needs. The way to Christ is through our real selves. The way to our true self is through Christ.

Growing in relationship with others in community is the third dimension of deepening. It is both a cause and a result of growing in relationship with God and self. In the community of faith we experience the love, correcting, and acceptance that bring a new dimension to God's love for us. Through this our relationship with God is enhanced and our ability to look honestly at ourselves grows. Also, however, the growth in our relationship with God provides the common bond that deepens the experience of community. And, similarly, growth in our relationship with self frees us from the self-centeredness that undercuts our ability to fully participate in the life together of the community.

Although writing to a wider and often secular audience, Parker Palmer has provided an image of such a community of faith. Rejecting what he sees to be the more common therapeutic, civic, and marketing models of community that predominate in today's culture, he advocates instead a community of truth. "The first step toward understanding the community of truth is to understand that community is the essential form of reality. . . ."[4] This is the audacious declaration the church makes when it claims to be the body of Christ, who is the Truth. It is only in and through this community—this body—that we participate in what is truly real and really true. It is the way, because of the power of Christ's resurrection, we experience things as they truly are, not the way they appear to be. Palmer goes on to say: "The next step takes us from the nature of reality to the question of how we know it: we know reality only by being in community with it ourselves."[5] It is only in the community of faith that we come to understand the reality of

Christ's presence in our lives and the truth that is Christ. This is the power that holds the community of truth together.

Dietrich Bonhoeffer, in writing about his years with an underground seminary in Nazi Germany, provides additional insight into the nature of Christian community. He affirms the interrelatedness of the three dimensions of deepening in language whose lack of inclusiveness betrays its age, but which nonetheless probes deeply. Although he does not draw strict distinctions between the three, the way in which they are all essential to each other becomes apparent as he writes of the need of Christians for each other:

> The Christian needs another Christian who speaks God's Word to him. He needs him again and again when he becomes uncertain and discouraged, for by himself he cannot help himself without belying the truth. He needs his brother man as a bearer and proclaimer of the divine word of salvation. He needs his brother solely because of Jesus Christ. The Christ in his own heart is weaker than the Christ in the word of his brother; his own heart is uncertain, his brother's is sure.[6]

And again as he writes of the importance of confession:

> Since the confession of sin is made in the presence of a Christian brother, the last stronghold of self-justification is abandoned. The sinner surrenders; he gives up all his evil. He gives his heart to God, and he finds the forgiveness of all his sin in the fellowship of Jesus Christ and his brother.[7]

Christ, community, and self are bound together. Deepening the relationship with all three is essential for those who would be disciples.

The early chapters of Acts provide a biblical illustration of this kind of deepening. First, there is the description of Pentecost in Acts 2:41–42: "So those who welcomed his message were baptized, and that day about three thousand were added. They devoted themselves to the apostles' teaching and fellowship, to the breaking of bread and the prayers." The new believers gathered together in community. They shared in spiritual disciplines to deepen their relationship with Christ. The disciplines described in these verses are both personal and corporate. They led to a deepening of both mind and spirit—through the study of Scripture that stimulates the mind and the experience of worship that touches the spirit. The passage also makes it clear that discipline is essential. The early disciples "devoted" themselves to these things. It was a commitment of time and self to be involved, to do the things that were needed in order to live out the transforming experience of Christ they had just had. This was not a one-day-a-week commitment, but one that shaped every day of their lives. These and other spiritual disciplines serve to enhance our relationship with Christ, encourage reflection that deepens our knowledge of ourselves, and provide a common experience that binds the community more tightly together.

There was also, quite clearly, the submission of self of which Carlyle Marney spoke. Without the offering up of self-directed images and needs, the intimacy of sharing described in verses 44–45 would not have been possible: "All who believed were together and had all things in common; they would sell their possessions and goods and distribute the proceeds to all, as any had need." Even if we do not follow these words literally, they point to a depth of relationship and caring that is only possible in a community in which people have found the ability to free themselves from self-centered concerns and begun to trust in their relationship with God and each other to provide for the essential needs of life.

EQUIPPING—GROWING IN GIFTEDNESS

The beginning point for our understanding of equipping is found in Ephesians 4:11–12: "The gifts [Christ] gave were that some would be apostles, some prophets, some evangelists, some pastors and teachers, to equip the saints for the work of ministry, for building up the body of Christ."

Gifts are central to equipping. They are the raw material given by God to each person. It is because believers are gifted that they are able to lead lives as faithful disciples. It is not their doing; it is God's work. It is not their effort; it is God's grace. That is where the gifts come from. And yet, there is a role for the disciple and the community to play. The gifts given by God need to be recognized or, to put it more accurately, they need to be called forth. This is one of the primary responsibilities of the Christian community— to call forth the gifts that God has given to its members so that all may be aware of the great resources that are available to do God's work. It doesn't stop with knowing about the gifts, however. The gifts, once they are known, need to be developed through both study and practice, in trial and testing. In this way the gifts are refined so that they can be used more effectively. In this way, disciples become more confident in the use of their gifts as they reach their full potential.

One of my most basic beliefs about our God-given gifts is that they are so much a part of us that we tend not even to be aware of them. They come so naturally to us that we think nothing of them. In fact, often our frustration at someone else's seeming inability to do something is not a matter of anything they lack at all; it is rather that we have a gift for this particular thing and it comes so easily and naturally to us that we assume everyone should be able to do it. This means, of course, that without someone around to tell us about these gifts we may live in ignorance about them. If that happens, we shortchange both God and ourselves, as well as run the risk of being unfairly critical of others. We shortchange God because without knowledge of these gifts we cannot develop and use them in ways that will contribute to God's intentions for us. We shortchange ourselves because we continue to operate out of a misunderstanding of who we are and the qualities that make us unique.

I discovered a gift that is vitally important to my ministry because someone in the community told me I had it. I didn't know it before. I didn't believe it when they told me. In fact, it took a number of people telling me over the period of a number of years before I believed that I was a creative person. I had always understood creativity to be something artists had—the quality that helped them paint or compose. I couldn't do any of that. But people kept telling me I was creative and I began to understand that this creativity was in the way I saw things, not in the things I made. I looked at things differently than most people. I was able to make connections between things that others couldn't. I saw relationships between things that others didn't see. Now, I admit that this one is not on the list of "spiritual gifts" that we see so often. Paul never talks about the gift of "seeing things differently" the way he talks about the gifts of tongues or interpretation. Perhaps it might be part of the gift of discernment, in that the ability to make these connections is vital to gaining insight into the best way to respond to a situation. But, whether it was on someone's list or not didn't really matter. Because the community saw this in me when I was blind to it, because the community began to rely on me to bring this gift to its life, I came to understand something of the way in which God had gifted me for the ministry God wanted me to perform.

All of us need the community of faith to call forth our gifts and provide the setting in which we can develop them—to our benefit and God's glory.

Even more, however, these gifts need to be directed in the right way. That is why our understanding of call is important. The gifts that come from God are to be used in living out the call that comes from God. Again, the help of the community of faith is essential. The community plays a vital role in helping discern the call, aiding believers as they sort through all the demands that are placed upon them so they can discover what God really wants them to be about. This call from God isn't to be seen as something alien to the person we are. It is not a call away from vitality in living. It is not a call to give up the essence of our being. It is, rather, a call to fulfill-ment—to fulfill God's intentions for us. Those intentions are not the same as our own wishes. Sometimes they may challenge the dreams we have for ourselves. Often they lead us to set aside other attractive possibilities. But God's intention for us is always to fulfill our true self. This sense of call is based in the faith that God put each one of us on earth for a purpose; that is why each one of us was created as the person we are. In responding to God's call we fulfill the intention of our creation and achieve a meaning to our living that is available to us in no other way. Gifts and call go hand in hand as one important dimension of equipping.

The second dimension of equipping is knowledge and skills. In order to be about God's work, disciples need to know and be able to do certain things. Some of these are common for everyone. All disciples need to know about the Bible and the life of faith. All need to know just what it is that makes one a disciple. All need to be able to engage in the basic practices of the faith—to worship and to pray, to give and to love. These are all things that can be learned—some in the classroom, some through careful reflection on living.

Additional knowledge and skills are specific to the call. A pastor needs to know and be able to do some different things than a teacher. A person who lives out God's call as a parent needs to know and be able to do some different things than one who lives it out as a carpenter or as Sunday school superintendent. Both common and specific knowledge and skills are essential to equipping. It is the responsibility of each disciple to acquire the skills and knowledge that are needed for faithful discipleship. It is the responsibility of the community to insure that all disciples are equipped to faithfully and effectively respond to God's call.

Equipping provides the direction for discipleship. It funnels our passion so that it is usable. It develops our gifts so that they are used to their potential. It attunes us to God's call so that we will direct our efforts in the way that God intends. It provides the skill and knowledge we need to be effective.

MINISTERING—GROWING IN SERVICE

A disciple always seeks to become more like the one he or she follows. For the Christian disciple that means becoming more like Jesus by becoming more fully engaged in God's work in creation. That was what the ministry of Jesus was about. It is what Christ's disciples are about as well. It is here that faith is put into action or, to use an image of Jesus, it is here that disciples bear the fruit of their discipleship. But this isn't just the end product of discipleship. It is also a way to continue to grow as disciples. This is the way James put it:

> But be doers of the word, and not merely hearers who deceive themselves. For if any are hearers of the word and not doers, they are like those who look at themselves in a mirror; for they look at themselves and, on going away, immediately forget what they were like. But those who look into the perfect law, the law of liberty

and persevere, being not hearers who forget but doers who act—
they will be blessed in their doing.

James 1:22–25

This is a striking image. Think about it for a minute. This is
how it often works in my life. I look in the mirror in the morning
as I shave and I know full well what I look like. The small mouth,
the double chin, the narrow eyes are all readily apparent. But then
I leave the bathroom and go about my daily work. By noon I can
easily convince myself that I really look a good bit like Robert
Redford. By dinner I find myself thinking that I am in all probabil-
ity a dead ringer for Brad Pitt!

That is how it works with faith, James is telling us. If faith isn't
put into action, it is easily forgotten—just as a person forgets the
details of his or her looks after walking away from a mirror. We can
easily delude ourselves into thinking that our faith is deeper or
stronger than it is. Or conversely, we can refuse to acknowledge the
true depth of our faith, believing it to be something less than it
truly is. Action makes the difference. It makes such delusions less
likely, because the Word has become flesh, embodied in the way
the disciple lives. We know how deep our faith is, how much it
really shapes our living because the evidence is right in front of us
every day.

Ministering is our active participation in God's mission. It can
happen wherever that mission is taking place. Since, as we have
already noted, God's mission is nothing less than the redemption
of all creation, our role as disciples is nothing less than active participation in redeeming creation.

In order to continue to enhance our growth as disciples, however, the action in ministering does not stand on its own. Rather, it
becomes the subject of ongoing reflection: What did I learn from
that experience? How were my gifts used? How did it strengthen or
challenge my sense of call? How did it deepen my relationship with
God? In what ways did it strengthen our sense of community?
Through reflection on questions such as these, ministering forms
disciples.

Before going further, we need to be clear about the dangers of
participation in this mission of God. We like to think it is simply a

matter of being kind and sharing love with others. We often see Jesus' ministry solely in those terms. That was part of it, to be sure. But it's quite unlikely, even in Roman times, that a man would be crucified for simply being kind and sharing love. Participation in God's mission of redeeming all creation can lead us into all manner of trouble. Sometimes it is a matter of being kind and sharing love, but at other times it means challenging the powers and principalities of this world. And that can be dangerous. Sometimes we are called to take bold and obvious risks. But at other times the danger comes not because we seek confrontation, but simply because we act in ways that are perceived by others to be threatening. Think about the simple act of Jesus in welcoming children, for example. This story (found in Luke 18:15–17) is viewed as a pleasant account of a kindly man—the stuff of Children's Day sermons. But consider this: what would happen today to a thirty-year-old unmarried man who went around saying, "Let the children come to me"? Sometimes the simple act of being kind can lead us into danger. Sharing in the ministry of Christ can be dangerous work. Often it isn't, but it can be. We should be clear about that from the beginning.

It is in ministering that I have experienced the greatest joys and greatest pains of my life. To be part of an experience that transforms others, that helps them see themselves and their lives in ways they never before thought possible, brings unparalleled joy. To share in experiences of giving in which you receive more than you could ever have imagined brings a sense of wondrous awe that simply cannot be expressed. And yet, to respond to God's call to ministry can also lead one into great struggle. For God's ministry is about truth telling, and many fear the truth and seek to discredit those who share it. God's ministry is about redeeming unhealthy, dysfunctional behaviors, and there are those who build their lives on these things and refuse to let them go. God's ministry is often about challenging the way things are in order to make the possibility of God's future more real, and there are those who will expend untold effort to keep things just the way they are. I dislike pain and conflict as much as anyone, and yet I have learned that ministry often involves both of these. I have also learned that it is in these times that the depth of relationship with God, self, and others in community, the awareness of our gifts, and the clarity of our call are crucially important. For these are things that bring us joy, even when the ministry itself brings pain.

THE RELATIONSHIP OF THE THREE ELEMENTS

We've talked about deepening, equipping, and ministering as if they are three distinct elements. That's helpful for a beginning understanding, but it does not give a true picture of how discipleship works in the real life of a congregation. There are profound and intricate relationships and interactions among all three. Each contributes to the other; each benefits from the other.

Engagement in ministering, for example, affects both deepening and equipping. Disciples grow in their relationship with Christ because they have shared Christ's ministry with him. They serve, as he did. At times they may suffer, as he did. At other times they experience the wonder of the new life of the resurrection, as he did. In similar fashion, ministering leads in profound ways to a greater self-understanding as one's strengths and weaknesses become more apparent in service to others. The sin that makes it difficult to move beyond our own needs and passions becomes more apparent as we attempt to live for others, as does the depth of our love. Ministering also enhances relationship in community—both as the community itself is engaged in ministry and as it offers support for those who are. In both cases ministering provides a concrete experience that can strengthen the bonds of community.

Ministering also affects equipping. Disciples become more fully equipped as they learn more about God's mission, about the gifts they have and need to develop further, about God's call and how they can respond to it, about the skills they have or need to acquire.

Similarly, experiences of deepening affect our experience of equipping and ministering, and experiences of equipping affect our experience of deepening and ministering. All are interrelated. Each one depends upon the others. All three are essential to the experience of the disciple from the very beginning. Together they provide the experience that enables us to keep growing as disciples. Deepening, equipping, and ministering are not three distinct and separate elements. This is not a three-course meal. Rather, it is a hearty soup in which each element retains its identity but is flavored by the others even as it flavors them. It is the mix of flavors that makes the soup.

Because these elements are so intimately tied together, it is important to avoid the inevitable tendency to think in terms of providing distinct experiences of deepening, equipping, and ministering—to say this week we will focus on deepening, next week on equipping, and the following week on ministering. When these are done best they are done with the awareness that all three elements are happening.

When the congregation itself plans experiences, it might be helpful to think in terms of a hologram. These wondrous three-dimensional pictures have a truly mysterious quality. Every piece of the hologram contains the whole. That means that if the hologram is broken into pieces, each piece is able to produce the entire hologram. That is a good image for developing disciple-forming experiences within the congregation. Each experience should contain the whole. Deepening, equipping, and ministering should be present everywhere.[8]

There is another significant by-product of living out the holistic understanding of discipleship that we have talked about. When deepening, equipping, and ministering are present in the life of a disciple-forming congregation, the long-standing tension between in-reach and outreach, between care for current members and mission to the unchurched, is significantly lessened, if not eliminated. It is impossible, with this understanding of discipleship, to form disciples of those who are already present in the congregation without at the very same time developing a vital program of outreach. Yes, their relationships with God and with each other will be deepened. Yes, there will be significant pastoral care, learning about the Bible, and developing spiritual disciplines. But this will happen at the same time that members are discerning their call to participate in God's mission in the world and being equipped with the skills and knowledge needed to respond to that call. The age-old tension between in-reach and outreach comes from a misunderstanding of the church's purpose as a disciple-forming community. When we grasp that purpose more fully, the tension decreases and we are able to affirm both as essential aspects of the church's mission. You simply cannot have one without the other.

Five ❖ The Disciple-Forming
Community: Practices

IT TAKES A COMMUNITY TO FORM A DISCIPLE. THE congregation exists to be that community. Children, youth, and adults together in the community of faith provide the resources that aid the forming of disciples. The Spirit present in that community provides the transforming power that makes disciples and encourages their continued growth. Without the community there can be no disciples. It is the community that carries the gospel story into the present so that it can be made real in the lives of disciples. It is the community that provides the variety of gifts that is essential to disciple formation. It is the community that offers the experiences of deepening, equipping, and ministering that form disciples.[1]

This needs to be said with humility, perhaps even confessionally. To make these statements is not to claim a privileged role for every congregation. It is, rather, a challenge to each local congregation, as part of the church universal, to live up to the expectations God has for the church. I don't read Jesus' declaration in Matthew 16:18 that the gates of Hell will not prevail against the church as a guarantee of eternal life for every local congregation, but as a word of challenge to be a disciple-forming community. That is the only way the gates of Hell won't prevail against us because that is the only way we can make any claim to being the church. When we cease to form disciples we cease to be the church and all bets are off. The guarantee here is not an institutional one; it is a functional one—God will always provide for the forming of disciples.

A WORD ABOUT EVANGELISM

Our focus in this book is on the congregation as a disciple-forming community. This is not to dismiss the importance of evangelism in the life of the church. In its broadest sense evangelism describes the work of the church with everyone before the commitment to Christ that makes him or her a disciple.[2] This means that most of our work with children and all our work with those who are unchurched is, in the strict sense, evangelism. It has as its purpose presenting the gospel in such a way that persons will claim its story as their story and make the commitment to Christ that leads to discipleship. Although the purpose of evangelism is different from that of discipleship, many of the experiences are the same. For one of the best ways to share the gospel with others is through experiences of deepening, equipping, and ministering. This is the way they learn about the Christian faith and what it means to follow Jesus. These are the experiences that lead them to want to become disciples.

There is also another direct connection between discipleship and evangelism. The gift and call of some disciples is to be evangelists. They need to be equipped with the skills and knowledge that are important for evangelism. The ministry they undertake is one of evangelism. There can be no evangelism without discipleship because evangelists are first of all disciples. But let us also be clear: not all disciples are evangelists. The gifts are many; the calls are diverse. To be sure, all disciples, through their ministering, share the love of Christ and the truth of the gospel with others. But only some do this deliberately and intentionally as evangelists.

AN INCLUSIVE COMMUNITY

It is important to remember that the disciple-forming community is an inclusive one. It is that, first of all, because it is open to all who come. Involvement in the life of the congregation comes with no preconditions. Membership assumes an intentional commitment to grow as a disciple, but involvement is for all who will come. There can be no artificial barriers of class, culture, ethnicity, race, sex, or age in the disciple-forming community, for that would deny the reality of God's mission of the redemption of all creation. That is an all-inclusive mission.

The community is inclusive, secondly, in that it takes seriously the processes of deepening, equipping, and ministering for all who are there. These experiences do not depend upon age or ability. They hold true for the youngest child and the oldest adult. Their validity is not lessened by any disability. The style and content of the experiences will of course vary according to these and other factors, but the elements themselves do not.

Think, for example, of the importance of deepening in the lives of children and the ways that impacts the disciple-forming community. Morton Kelsey states the matter plainly when he says: "We can only educate our children spiritually . . . as we provide growing, knowledgeable, and mature adult parents and teachers to guide them, to share with them, and to exemplify genuine . . . spiritual wisdom."[3] Effective discipleship with children is only possible when effective discipleship with adults is happening. We cannot help children grow as disciples unless we ourselves are growing disciples. "If children are to learn to relate to the Holy One, they need to be led by parents and teachers who have learned to pray, to meditate, to relate to the Divine Lover. We need to worship together, and we also need to have our private times of communication with the Holy One."[4]

We should not underestimate the importance of the spiritual experiences and theological thinking that are already a part of children's lives. Ronald Cram critiques the church for not taking these as seriously as it should and assuming that children simply need to be told about faith. When he asked his 12 year-old son, for example, about his Sunday school class and whether or not he shared his thoughts about God, his son replied, "Oh, no! They would just tell me I was wrong or something." He then asked, "Ben, has anyone at church ever asked you about God, what you think about God?" Ben replied, "No, never. They just tell me what to think."[5]

Cram makes a number of suggestions regarding the implications of these insights. Two are particularly important to us:

> The first step of any program of Christian religious education or evangelism is not proclamation but listening. As teachers, we need to remember that the various texts of theological reflection already at work among children are a form of knowledge that is far more durable and practical than most of what goes on in formal church program settings.
>
> The primary focus of the evangelist or Christian religious educator needs to shift from the concern with children getting the Christian stories "right" to understanding that the primary responsibility of the teacher is to listen attentively for the ways in which children are interpreting the Christian stories in their times and in their places. The real curriculum of Christian religious education is not to be understood as the stories or materials that the teacher presents to the child. Rather, the real curriculum is what is developed in the conversations about faith and meaning that take place between the student and the teacher."[6]

The key to the congregation's ability to enhance the experiences of deepening in the lives of children rests in the vitality of faith among adults in the community. Their own experiences of deepening must be real and mature. They need the ability to help children reflect on their experiences and relate these to Christian understandings of God and, perhaps even more importantly, relate them to the community's experience of God in its midst.

Or again, consider the importance of equipping in the lives and faith development of youth. In a chapter entitled "Giftedness: A Unique Faith-Shaping Agenda" in *Faith Shaping: Youth and the Experience of Faith,* Stephen Jones suggests one method of enhancing the experience of equipping with youth. The essence of his argument is: "If youth understand their talents, resources, and abilities as gifts (not 'I am talented' but 'I am gifted'), then the unfolding of God's gift is a matter of faith development."[7] This approach to equipping with youth recognizes that shaping identity is their primary developmental task. It seeks to frame an answer to the question "Who am I?" in ways that are both personally meaningful and that enhance faith understanding.

As youth work through the great variety of issues involved in shaping their identity, they are very much aware of personal qualities that differentiate them from others. They naturally focus on the things they do well, both as a way to demonstrate their competency and as a way to make a statement about who they are as persons. A perspective that faith brings to this process is the understanding that these "things I do well" are, in fact, gifts from God. They are a part of the person God created you to be. They are the basis upon which you will live out God's intentions for you in life. As we make this theological connection to the developmental task, identity formation is seen as an issue of faith development.

Community is essential for the growth of a sense of giftedness in youth. It is the community that, in many cases, makes youth aware of the gifts that God has given. It is the community that helps youth understand these qualities as gifts—and for which our primary emotion should be thanksgiving, not pride. It is also the community that provides the setting in which the gifts can begin to be used. This use of gifts aids in their development. It also leads youth to another concern of equipping, discerning one's call. Call and gifts are intimately tied together. Through the use of gifts youth begin to sort through what they do well and what they do not, what they enjoy and what they do not, what things bring them a sense of fulfillment and what things do not. This is the raw material out of which a sense of call is fashioned. When concerns about God's work in our lives and God's intentions for us are brought to this raw material it becomes possible to discern God's call.

Stop now and reread these last few paragraphs. Each time the word children or youth appears substitute adult. While there will be some exceptions, in most cases the validity of the statements remains. There are differences in development and experience, but the concept of forming disciples through experiences of deepening, equipping, and ministering is valid for all ages. This is how disciples are formed.

PRACTICES

More than anything else disciple forming is an enculturation process. Discipleship cannot just be taught; it has to be lived. For that reason the practices of the congregation play a vitally important role in disciple-forming.

In some respects the intentional look at practices and what they teach is a new area of interest for many congregations. One of the consequences of modernity was an operating assumption that classroom learning could provide most, if not all, a person needed to know to be a Christian. Content was what mattered—especially content that could be communicated within the confines of an easy-to-use curriculum. So, new member classes shared information about the church and the denomination, and "discipling" new Christians meant telling them what Christians should believe about important matters of faith. We opted for the modern belief that if people could understand the right things they would then live the right way.

One of the great blessings of the postmodern world is that it has enabled us to move beyond this "head tripping" about faith and recover the importance of practice in forming disciples. It's not that congregations didn't engage in practices during modernity, for that's always been the way people have really learned the lessons of faith and life. Rather, because we were less than clear about the importance of practice and less aware of the practices we were actually engaged in, we sometimes didn't practice what we preached.

Recent secular scholarship has described the learning process that takes place in the lives of people, placing great emphasis on the social nature of learning and the importance of developing practices through which people learn. Etienne Wenger, in *Communities of Practice: Learning, Meaning, and Identity,* focused on an insurance claims department to demonstrate that the knowledge that was essential to performing the job was acquired in a social context around a set of practices that established a learning community. It is not too much of a stretch to understand how, in a congregation, the knowledge that is essential to living as a Christian is acquired in a social context around a set of practices that establish a learning community. That learning community is the disciple-forming congregation.

A few additional insights from secular writing will help us get a clearer picture of what goes on in such a community. Wenger notes that, even in a business setting, not everything that is essential to effective functioning can be codified, described, and placed in a manual. Tacit knowledge is essential. The sharing of tacit knowledge requires "interaction and informal learning processes such as storytelling, conversation, coaching, and apprenticeship."[8] Think for a minute about how this is even truer for those seeking to live as faithful disciples. The knowledge it takes to do that certainly cannot be fully contained in a manual! It requires something more. Through the ages the church has recognized the reality of that "something more" by making storytelling, conversation, coaching, and apprenticeship an important part of the life of the community of faith. Indeed, the Bible itself relies on storytelling to convey its message about what it means to live as a faithful people. To form disciples today we need to be even more intentional about the practices that are needed.

One additional insight will be helpful to us. According to Wenger, every effective learning community contains three elements: a domain, a community, and a practice.[9] The domain is the area of common concern that brings people together—for the church this is the gospel of Jesus Christ. The community provides the context for learning. "It encourages a willingness to share ideas, expose one's ignorance, ask difficult questions, and listen carefully."[10] This is the congregation, living as the body of Christ. The practice is the "set of frameworks, tools, information, styles, language, stories and documents"[11] that is needed for effective functioning in the domain. This is the "stuff" of disciple-forming—all those things that are a part of the life of the community that aid disciples in living more faithfully. In our framework of deepening, equipping, and ministering, it is all those things that happen within the congregation that make these possible. Note that this is a bit different from the traditional understanding of Christian practices, which usually refers to specific spiritual formation disciplines. Those disciplines are part of the practice in the sense that it is used here.

So, what about Christian practice today and how does being a "community of practice" aid the congregation in becoming a disciple-forming community?

The best way to get a handle on this will be to look at some specific examples of the way it happens. We'll use four different authors to guide us on this part of our journey. Diana Butler Bass, in *The Practicing Congregation: Imagining a New Old Church,* will help us look at the way in which the recovery of traditional Christian practices has been the key to revitalization in some congregations. Craig Dykstra, in *Growing in the Life of Faith: Education and Christian Practices,* will help us explore some specific practices he believes have been an important part of the life of the church, sometimes without us even realizing it. Dorothy Bass, the editor of *Practicing Our Faith: A Way of Life for a Searching People,* will point out a number of nontraditional practices that can shape our lives as disciples. And finally, Doug Pagitt in *Reimagining Church: A Week in the Life of an Experimental Church,* will take us on a tour of the spiritual practices they are using in his new church start.

One way to become a Christian community of practice is through the reinvigoration of traditional Christian practices, allowing these to shape the life and faith of the congregation. Diana Butler Bass sees these practices as falling into four broad areas: worship, prayer, moral formation, and life together.[12] Recognizing the "collective amnesia" of contemporary society in which we forget our identity and purpose, she notes

> Christian communities can no longer assume that congregants know their story; it must be imaginatively told, retold, and enacted, so that tradition becomes a living thing. Practicing congregations are dynamic learning communities in which this process occurs. These churches model a particular way of life; communities of practice that forge, express, and bear certain traditions.[13]

It is through this process of recovery of practices that the story comes alive in the lives of today's disciples. They see more clearly and follow more nearly because they have been able to live out the meaning of faithfulness in their participation in the congregation. It's not necessarily an easy transition for congregations to make, however. For those congregations who have made this journey it has meant giving up an institutional view of the church in order to "provide a kind of spiritual entry point into creative new patterns of being church . . . [based in] appropriating and reworking traditions and practices that met contemporary challenges."[14]

Seeing the need to revitalize traditional and develop new disciplined practices of faith, Craig Dykstra expands our view of spiritual practices that enhance disciple formation. He looks more broadly at the life of the congregation and points out activities in which congregations engage that emerge from our faith. He names fourteen of these that are both consistent and significant in congregations:

- worshiping God together
- telling the Christian story to one another
- interpreting together the Scriptures and the history of the church's experience
- praying
- confessing our sin to one another
- tolerating one another's failures and encouraging one another
- carrying out specific faithful acts of service and witness
- giving generously
- suffering with and for one another and all our neighbors
- providing hospitality and care
- listening and talking attentively to one another
- struggling together to become conscious of and to understand the world in which we live
- criticizing and resisting powers and patterns that destroy people and corrode community
- working together to maintain and create structures and institutions that sustain life[15]

Some of these, such as worship, are formal, traditional practices. Others, such as tolerating one another, while certainly a part of most Christian communities, don't typically appear on official lists of spiritual disciplines! All of these together, however, provide a template for looking at the life of a congregation in order to lift up those practices that enhance faithful discipleship, to be more intentional about creating them and more deliberate about making the best possible use of them. Knowing, for example, that our ability to tolerate each others' failings is both an expression of our faith and a means of growing in the life of faith can help a congregation claim its identity as a disciple-forming community.

The insights brought together by Dorothy Bass further expand our understanding of the practices of faith that enhance our growth as disciples. *Practicing Our Faith* provides another selection of life activities, which, seen from the perspective of faith, provide the congregation with new opportunities for forming disciples. While there is some overlap with Dykstra, this list also brings some important new perspectives. What is important in these practices, according to Bass, is to do the ordinary things of life well and faithfully.[16] These are the ordinary things of life upon which she focuses her attention:

- honoring the body
- hospitality
- household economics
- saying yes and saying no
- keeping Sabbath
- testimony
- discernment
- shaping communities
- forgiveness
- healing
- dying well
- singing our lives

In the community of faith all of these are infused with two traditional Christian practices. Prayer and Bible study are always essential. Without them all of the other practices collapse of their own weight, for the vitality that gives them life is lacking.

Imagine being able to start all over again. That's what it was like for Doug Pagitt and the members of Solomon's Porch, a new church start in Minneapolis. Without specific practices from the history of their congregation, they were able to focus primarily on the development of ones that would have particular meaning for their time and place and people. Here's what they came up with:

* worship
* physicality
* dialogue
* hospitality
* belief
* creativity
* service

Some of these look familiar; others may seem strange. All of them, however, provide ways in which those who participate in them can live out the Christian faith in specific ways within a community. This is particularly important for Solomon's Porch, which is committed to reaching out to those in its area who are not Christians. For those people practices are especially important.

> Most people come to faith . . . through living day by day with people of faith such as their families or friends. People may not fully understand the beliefs involved, but they learn what the Christian life looks like as they see people to whom they are deeply connected living out the disciplines of prayer, worship and service. . . .
>
> Community as a means of spiritual formation serves to immerse people in the Christian way of living so that they learn how to be Christian in a life-long process of discovery and change.[17]

This "life-long process of discovery and change" is what discipleship is all about. It is the way disciples are formed. It is the task of the community of faith. It is accomplished as that community provides opportunities for deepening, equipping, and ministering in the practices it adopts.

Our four tour guides have left us with much to ponder and process. There is an array of practices—formal and less so, traditional and less so—available to the congregation as it seeks to live out the challenge to form disciples. The particular practices a congregation chooses will depend on its own way of faithfulness and the people it is seeking to involve. It is always important, however, to think in terms of practices when we think about forming disciples. Book learning, classroom teaching, dynamic preaching isn't enough. Practice—the living out of faith in disciplined ways—may not make perfect, but it is essential.

Deepening, equipping, and ministering happen through the practices of faith. While some practices may focus on one of these more than the others, virtually all of them encompass all three elements of discipleship to some extent. There are not deepening practices, equipping practices, and ministering practices; there are only discipleship practices. When the community of faith is intentional about its practices, people grow in faith and discipleship. And the disciple-forming community becomes a reality.

Six ❖ The Disciple-Forming Community: Qualities

Disciple forming isn't about establishing a new program. It doesn't happen if it is the responsibility of one of the church boards. It is only possible if it is the vision that guides the entire congregation and infuses every aspect of the congregation's life and ministry. It is as much a matter of structure as it is program, as much a concern for building use as it is community involvement. As we noted in the previous chapter, it happens not so much through what is taught as through the practices of the community—the way faith is lived out both within and outside the church.

The question for us then becomes: what are the qualities of a community of faith that most encourage these disciple-forming practices? As we answer that question let's state the obvious first. Each disciple-forming community is unique; there is no one model that can be applied to every congregation. That means that each congregation needs to find its way to being a disciple-forming community. What works for First Baptist won't be the answer for First Presbyterian or for the Community Church, even though they may be located in the same community. There are no gimmicks that will guarantee success, no books that can tell you what to do. Each congregation needs to discover its own sense of community, attune itself to the Spirit's presence in its midst, and discern God's will for its life and ministry. As it does that, the disciple-forming community God has called it to be will begin to emerge. And it will be unique.

But there is more to it than that. It is not simply a matter of striking out on your own to see what you might discover along the way. There are a number of qualities that are generally present in churches that are discovering the vitality that comes with being a disciple-forming community. Not every church has all of them. Not all of them may be valid for your congregation. But they do provide a place to begin. Being aware of them provides a sensitivity that is needed as a congregation begins to discover what shape its disciple-forming community will take. Let's take a look at these qualities now.[1]

SPIRITUAL VITALITY

A disciple-forming congregation is a contagious place of spiritual growth. It is a place where the movement of God's Spirit is obvious in the lives of individuals and the whole body. The congregation and its people have a passion to be what God has called them to be. Their life together is shaped by a desire to grow in relationship with Christ so that they may discern God's call to them more fully.

This is the essential quality of the disciple-forming congregation. Without this all the other qualities lose their potency and become nothing more than a checklist of things to do.

A church cannot be a church without spiritual vitality.[2] A disciple cannot be a disciple without spiritual vitality. It may come in many forms, it may be based in a variety of practices, but spiritual vitality is essential. Rather than define that vitality, let's try to describe what it might look like. Here are some of the characteristics of churches where I have sensed a genuine spiritual vitality:

♦ There is an abiding desire to grow in relationship with Christ.
♦ There is an active trust in the power of God.

+ There is an evident sense of humility.
+ There is a deep yearning to discern and respond to God's call.
+ There is a willingness to change.
+ There is an ability to deal with the conflict that change inevitably brings.
+ There is an enduring spirit of gentleness.
+ There is a bold commitment to participate in God's mission in the world, often in a prophetic way.

In the disciple-forming community these are both personal and corporate qualities. Individual disciples can be described this way. The congregation as a whole can be described this way.

This spiritual vitality has its foundation in Christ. It is Christ who brings the passion for such a life. It is Christ who makes such a life possible. So it is in our relationship with Christ that our discipleship is formed and lived.

There are few who have demonstrated the life of discipleship more clearly in recent years than Mother Teresa. A story from her life illustrates the essential nature of this relationship with Christ, even for those whose discipleship is lived out in less dramatic fashion. Mother Teresa was on a speaking tour of North America at the time. This is how Ernest Boyer tells the story.

> Among the groups to which she spoke was one of religious sisters from many North American orders. After her talk she asked if there were any questions.
>
> "Yes, I have one," a woman sitting near the front said. "As you know, most of the orders represented here have been losing members. It seems that more and more women are leaving all the time. And yet your order is attracting thousand upon thousand. What do you do?"
>
> Without hesitating Mother Teresa answered, "I give them Jesus."
>
> "Yes I know, but take habits, for example. Do your women object to wearing habits? And the rules of the order, how do you do it?"
>
> "I give them Jesus."

"Yes, I know Mother, but can you be more specific."

"I give them Jesus."

"Mother, we are all of us aware of your fine work. I want to know about something else."

"I give them Jesus. There is nothing else."[3]

"I give them Jesus. There is nothing else." This is the basis upon which disciples live their lives. Disciples understand that without Jesus it is impossible to be the persons God created them to be. Disciple-forming congregations understand that without Jesus it is impossible to form disciples. Both understand that without Jesus there is nothing else.

Disciple forming is an impossible task—if we rely simply on our skills and efforts. What makes it possible is the presence of Christ's Spirit at work in a congregation. It is the Spirit that gives the vision. It is the Spirit that provides the passion. It is the Spirit that guides the way. Without the Spirit we are reduced to going through the motions or completing the checklist of things we are supposed to do. Without the Spirit, we can never get it right!

The foundation for everything else that happens in the disciple-forming community is a passion to be the congregation God has called it to be. Individually, people are motivated by the desire to discover and respond to God's call in their lives—to live out the purpose for which God has created them. Corporately, the congregation seeks to be the church that God has called it to be in its particular time and place. Without these two forces providing the motivation, discipleship remains shallow and disciple forming lacks potency.

This spiritual vitality touches every aspect of the life of the disciple-forming congregation. Leaders continually seek a deeper awareness of God's presence in their lives. Small groups strive to become communities in which Christ's presence is made real. Worship is about the praise of God for God's presence and power at work in the world.

This spiritual vitality, of necessity, moves people and the congregation beyond an exclusive concern for personal, individual salvation in order to partake of the full array of blessings that God has provided—in both this world and the next. It is about abundant living based in loving relationships directed by an abiding sense of God's presence and power. It is about being Christ for others in a world in desperate need of peace, joy, hope, justice, and love. It touches every aspect of life: personal, family, work, community, and church.

This spiritual vitality cannot be manufactured. There is no list of steps that lead to guaranteed results. It is solely up to God. What the congregation can do, however, is continually seek to open itself to God and the work God is about in its midst. This is not an easy thing to do. It demands discipline—in Bible study and prayer. It often requires letting go of our past in order to embrace God's future. It usually necessitates setting aside what "we" want from "our" church and discovering what God wants from Christ's church. Any congregation that engages in the process will meet uncertainty, struggle, and conflict. But—and this is a great and wondrous but— the demands that the search for spiritual vitality place upon us pale in comparison to the ways in which it transforms both people and congregation. If there is struggle, then surely there is comfort. If there is death, then surely there is resurrection. With that resurrection comes new life—a life that finds deeper purpose, richer meaning, and more profound hope. And that is when spiritual discipline becomes spiritual vitality!

This focus on spiritual vitality is one of the ways disciple forming speaks directly to the postmodern world. As we have moved away from modernity's concern for scientific objectivity, spiritual concerns have become heightened. It is as if something is telling us there is more to life than what science can prove, more to knowing how to live than objective knowledge. This has led to a profound search for spiritual reality. It has taken many forms, from New Age channeling to Eastern mysticism. It has also provided the setting in which the church has been led to reclaim its own spiritual foundations. As congregations enhance their spiritual vitality, they can more effectively meet the needs of those who are on a spiritual search. But beware! It won't work if it is just a technique for reaching people, for adding new members. It will only work if it is a genuine expression of a reality in the lives of the people of the congregation. There is no room for shallowness here; no room for a play acting spirituality of pious language.

My own journey as a disciple is grounded in the desire for such spiritual vitality. I have to admit that I have not always found it in the church, even in churches in which I was the pastor. Somehow, amidst all the board meetings and program planning, it has often been difficult to live out the kind of spiritual vitality I know is so essential. I've maintained at least a semblance of it through my personal spiritual disciplines, but it has been more difficult to make it an ongoing corporate experience. One of the leaders in a church I served once shared her own struggle with this. She acknowledged that although this was her church and she loved the people in it, when she had deep spiritual needs that had to be met she went elsewhere. Her honesty shocked me. It also awakened me to what I have come to believe is a much more widespread reality in congregations. All too often, even loyal and long-time members are not finding it easy (or even possible) to find the spiritual vitality they seek in their faith. There is a great need for us to create a setting that nurtures this spiritual vitality by encouraging those who seek it to join with others. One of the important aspects of my own life over the past several years, for example, has been two different groups that have met regularly to support each other in our life pursuits and challenges as we seek God's presence and leading. We continue to find better ways to do that (and at times it is, in all honesty, difficult to maintain), but we continue because we share a deeply felt common need that must be met. We don't need direction from a congregation, just an environment in which it is possible to find each other and which encourages us to keep at it.

VITAL, TRANSFORMING WORSHIP

Disciple-forming congregations recognize that worship is an essential dimension of human life. They provide authentic experiences of worship for all—experiences that offer opportunities for praise, reflection, and celebration. Worship in the disciple-forming congregation is of and by the people, engaging them in experiences in which they are touched by the holy power of God so that they may know God more deeply and serve God more fully.

It is time to free worship from the shackles of personal ego and organizational need. It's time to make worship something other than the congregation's primary vehicle for education and/or evangelism. It's time to make it something more than the weekly event in which announcements are made, the sick list is shared and the choir performs. It's time to make the standard by which we evaluate worship something other than individual biases about music styles and the pastor's preaching. It is time to recover the transforming power of worship that provides an encounter with the holy!

Tom Bandy describes the experience of a fictional couple, Bob and Sally, as they attend worship for the first time. They are warmly greeted, their children are well and safely provided for, they encounter words and music that are familiar, they are emotionally and intellectually engaged.

> By the end of the service, Bob and Sally may not remember any particular scripture or idea. They may not "know" much more about doctrines, ethical demands, political ideologies, or organizational practices than they did before. . . . The point is that Bob and Sally have begun to observe, and to personally experience, the transforming power of God that can change people.[4]

There are other worship services offered by this church, as well—some more traditional or liturgical. However, "every one of them will nurture positive personal change, and every one of them will motivate people like Bob and Sally to disciplined learning, sharing, and mission through the week."[5]

The "worship wars" of recent years have tended to be about style. This misses the point. The real issue is whether or not worship offers an encounter with the holy, an opportunity to be touched by the transforming power of God. It is that power that makes personal change possible and motivates people to the learning, sharing, and mission that are the disciple's life. It does this not through cheerleading or guilt or persistence or example. It does it through the passion created by an encounter with the holy.

The issue for each congregation is whether or not this describes what happens in its services of worship—to both regular participants and newcomers. It's time to ask a difficult question and give an honest answer: on any given Sunday how many worshipers in your church would say they had experienced the holy? If the answer is something less than you want it to be, change is in order.

There is probably no aspect of a congregation's life in which there is more emotional investment than worship. Much of this is because worship is about the holy, and holy things are important to people. Some of this emotional investment may be based in misplaced or truncated understandings of the holy. Some of it may be based in inappropriate ego needs, extreme continuity needs, or just plain stubbornness. Whatever the cause, however, the emotional investment many have in worship often means that change can be difficult and often results in conflict. Because this is so, moving slowly while staying committed is one of the best ways to approach change in worship. I encourage people to CREEP as they do this: Consider the purpose, Recover the corporate, Explore the indigenous, Experiment with change, and Pray for openness.

Consider the purpose. Because the worship service is one of the few occasions that congregations gather in significant numbers, it has become the vehicle for accomplishing a wide range of important tasks that are not worship related. In many congregations it also serves fellowship needs, information-sharing needs, intercessory prayer needs, money-raising needs, teaching needs, performance needs, political needs, and an array of program support needs. Many of these are important to the life of a congregation. None of them, however, serve the purpose of worship. Leander Keck, in criticizing the secularization of worship, issues a call for a return to its essential purpose: the praise of God. His words remind us of the importance of praise and call us to refocus our worship services on this essential purpose.

> Praise is an oral activity, whether in speech or song, which acknowledges a superlative quality (like patience or beauty), or a deed (like a heroic rescue). It is more than an attitude of appreciation or an emotion like delight, although it usually includes elements of both . . . . Praise does not express a yearning or wish but responds to something given to us.[6]
>
> To praise the Creator is to acknowledge joyously, not grudgingly, that we did not make ourselves but are contingent on the One who cannot and must not be reduced to the guarantor of our

cultures and causes, however noble their aims and achievements. . . . God is to be praised because God is God, because of what God is and does, quite apart from what God is and does for me.[7]

There are indeed positive, constructive, liberating, healing, and enlightening consequences of the worship of God. We do get perspective on ourselves and the world, and we do become motivated to address its wrongs. But the utilitarian mind gets the priorities wrong by making the by-product the main product. It forgets, and perhaps denies, that the worship of God is an end in itself. If praise is the heart of worship, then making worship useful destroys it, because this introduces an ulterior motive for praise.[8]

Yes, worship should be vital and transforming for those who participate in it. But it can only be that when its focus is not on those participants and their needs or hopes or desires, but the praise and presence of God.

The implications of this simple insight are profound. What does it say about a sermon the purpose of which is to teach people about God or how to live a godly life? What does it say about prayers that offer our requests to God? The solution is certainly not to remove sermons and prayers from worship but to practice them in a new light—to preach in praise of God's Word and the way it touches our lives, to pray in praise of God's power and the way it responds to human need. Neither is the solution simply to sing a medley of songs that have praise in the titles. As Keck tells us, praise is a matter of both word and way. One of the greatest ways we offer praise to God is to participate in God's work in the world. Worship has a role to play in that, too, as it motivates us to go into the world, just as the Spirit motivated movement into the world at Pentecost. But in all things about worship, it is praise that should be our focus.

Recover the corporate. Worship is the work of the people, not the performance of the preacher or the choir. It is by its very nature participatory. The forms of worship that are common in many churches undercut participation. It is often limited to prescribed prayers or litanies. These in themselves can be very positive, but participation should not be limited to them.

One of the major forces at work to limit the corporate nature of worship is time. The full schedule of the pastor, with the great variety of demands that are placed upon her or him, encourages the adoption of a "plug-in" style of worship. It is easy to have a set order of worship comprised of discrete elements. With just a minimum of coordination around theme, each person can independently prepare those elements for which he or she is responsible, and on Sunday morning everything fits together nicely. This, however, does not enhance participation or lead to a true sense of corporate worship.

Corporate worship begins with corporate preparation. This will take time. It will necessitate dropping items from an already full schedule. It will require the recruitment and commitment of others to be part of a worship team. But this is the best way to recover corporate worship. Ideally that team will play a major role in both planning and leading worship. It will be a good representation of the congregation. It will be creative and include people with musical, artistic, and dramatic skills. It will allow its work to be shaped by the Word. It will offer itself to God in prayer.

Explore the indigenous. Worship expression is a two-way street. It is essential that the traditions of the church and the idioms of the culture meet on that street. Two thousand years of Christian worship have provided a rich tradition from which all of us can learn. Contemporary styles of expression and communication also provide a rich resource for worship. This is as it has always been. The traditions that have been passed down across the centuries were once the product of the culture in which they arose. The contemporary idiom shaped them and they continued to evolve as they interacted with new settings and cultural expressions. Even the oldest of our faith traditions have evolved through their ongoing interaction with successive cultures. In fact, the only ones that have not are the relatively new "traditions" that were developed out of the cultural milieu of the last century. In many cases, however, these are the traditions that shape the understanding of appropriate worship in congregations. Opinions about worship style, music, even which version of the Bible should be used are based not on the rich tradition of the church at worship, but the life experience of one or two generations. Certainly one challenge we face is to move beyond this relatively short-term experience and recover a deeper tradition that has been present in the church for centuries.

Perhaps the greatest challenge for us today, however, is discovering ways to incorporate the idioms of the new technological culture into worship. Michael Slaughter points out just how significant this development is:

> The Protestant Reformation was a movement of God's Spirit that rode the wave of the latest technology: the printing press. Printing was invented in Europe by Johannes Gutenberg between 1440 and 1456. Printing ushered in the age of literacy. Martin Luther seized the medium and in so doing "spoke the language of the culture." . . . Electronic media is to the "Reformation" of the twenty-first century what Gutenberg's press was to the Reformation of the sixteenth and seventeenth centuries . . . . The New Reformation will speak the language of the culture and employ the communication technology that shapes the culture.
>
> It might seem too strong to say that there is no alternative for the viability of the future of the Church, but I mean to be even more bold in claiming that the Media Reformation is a life or death issue for the Church.[9]

If Slaughter is correct, as I believe he is, the changes that are taking place in our culture because of the development of electronic media are also bringing profound changes to the way we as individuals think about things and interact with each other. That kind of change forces us to think deeply about ways we can best communicate in the new world that is coming into being.

Indigenous worship is worship that uses the idioms of culture and the traditions of faith to facilitate the experience of the holy.

Experiment with change. A style of experimentation should be encouraged in worship. Not experimentation for the sake of doing something different, but experimentation for the sake of worshiping more fully. There will be those who want it just the way it has always been. There may even be battles over such seemingly minor issues as whether or not to sing "amen" at the end of hymns. But don't give up hope. It is possible to develop a style of experimentation, making temporary adjustments in worship to see what happens. These changes should be preceded by discussion about the purpose of worship, but not by debate about what changes to institute. In many cases these need to be experienced before they can be talked about, so our approach to experimentation should be an activist one. These changes should happen in a context that affirms that a disciple is always growing in relationship with Christ and that part of growing is changing.

This "experimental" approach has several advantages. It permits changes to occur. It lessens the threat that comes with the prospect of permanent change. It creates flexibility, making worship less dependent upon doing the same thing every week. It begins to create flexibility on the part of worshipers. Over time it has the potential to lead to substantive change.

Not all change can be implemented this way, of course. There will come a time when there is nothing left to do but take a big and permanent leap of faith. Installing state-of-the-art technology, for example, cannot be done gradually or on a temporary basis. It calls for a significant and lasting commitment. But even this type of change can be less difficult if it is set in a context that has learned the value of experimenting and has allowed the time needed for people to understand why such a change is important to participation in God's mission.

Pray for openness. Prayer needs to be the constant in this process of change. Prayer for openness is particularly important—openness to God, to others, to new ways. If that kind of openness is present, worship wars don't happen. If that kind of openness is present, the congregation is led into experiences of worship that are vital and transforming. In this time of postmodern transition, with its great uncertainties and dislocations, worship can provide the experience that both grounds us and gives us hope. It does this not through making sense or even offering the comfort that comes with familiarity. It does this only as it enables us to encounter God.

Even CREEPing change in worship will, in many cases, bring stress and dissatisfaction. It may even lead to some people leaving the church because they do not want change at all. This is never easy, but with sensitivity to the people involved and concern for the new people you will be able to reach, change in worship is not only possible, it can be life-transforming.

A Focus on God's Mission

Disciple-forming congregations are mission stations. They understand that faithfully serving God is, first, a commitment to ministry to their community and world. Decisions about ministry, finances, staff, buildings, involvement of laity, and everything else in the congregation are based upon what best aids God's mission.

It might seem that a congregation that sees itself as a disciple-forming community is inwardly focused because its concern is the continual forming of those who are there into more faithful disciples. That is not the case, however. The disciple-forming congregation is focused on mission. It exists, ultimately, not for those who are there, but for those who are not. This is true because the disciples it is forming are being formed to share in God's mission of the redemption of all creation. Disciples are missionaries. Disciple-forming congregations are mission stations. This focus on mission takes on the challenge of the Great Commission in Matthew 28:18–20, not just for those already in the community of faith, but also those in the secular community in which the congregation is situated.

There may be no single greater way to impact the life of a congregation than to instill this focus on mission. It literally changes everything. It demands change in how people spend their time, in how the church building is used, and in the priorities that are set for the pastor. People live out their discipleship, not through service on boards, but in service to others. The building is less a gathering place and more a sending place. The pastor spends less time caring for members and more time equipping them.

A focus on mission moves the congregation away from a concern for structure and maintenance. The concern for institutional survival loses its potency, even in times of tight budgets and property woes. The prevailing concern is, "What has God called us to do and be for others in this particular time and place?"

This focus, of course, does not discount the legitimate needs, hurts, and sorrows of members of the faith community. But it does place dealing with them in a different perspective. It encourages us to see the meeting of needs, the healing of hurts, and the soothing of sorrows not just as ends in themselves, but also as ways to enhance mission. They are ways we grow as persons of faith so that we become more able to respond to God's call to serve others, both as individuals and as a community. The needs, hurts, and sorrows are also seen as experiences through which we enhance our mission because they are bonds that connect us to a needy, hurting, sorrowful world.

When I first encountered this notion about mission it troubled me. It seemed as if people already in the congregation were being treated as objects. Even pastoral care seemed to have an ulterior motive. It wasn't to help the people involved, but rather to get them ready to do the work of the church. The whole thing seemed pretty inconsiderate and uncaring. But then I remembered Jesus' words about losing our lives so that we could find them, and I realized that this was what was happening here. It is when we move out of concern for ourselves and into the healthy serving of others that we find our true self and genuine healing takes place. It is when we move to mission that pastoral care is most effective. That means that as we encourage people to prepare themselves to move out in concern for others we are supporting them in their own growth, we are demonstrating genuine care for them. It isn't a question of using them at all, but of genuinely and deeply caring for them. Jesus' words defy the old either/or notions about either caring for ourselves or for others, as if these were two totally separate activities. His words help us understand that the two cannot be separated.

A focus on mission requires great faith, because mission is costly. It doesn't immediately and quickly translate into new members and new givers. It will worry and perhaps deeply upset those whose concern is the financial viability of the institution, because there is no apparent return on investment. It will require the congregation to think differently about the legitimate reasons for going into debt. Mortgages for capital improvements are often acceptable to congregations, for example, but what about taking on debt in order to establish a capital funding pool to support mission?

Paul Nixon states the case clearly:

If I have learned one thing about the relationship between churches and their communities in the years since I embarked on this journey of pastoral ministry, it would have to be this: for a church to make a difference in the life of a community, it has to plant itself squarely in the center of community life. This planting is more than simply a matter of building location. It is more than providing an array of "outreach" programs. It is something that must go to the heart [of] the church's identity. The burning issues that drive the church forward must be issues that go to the heart of the community's needs. A church must understand that its constituency is not its membership. Members represent simply the inner circle of leadership. A church's primary constituency must be the wider community of people in which it lives.

At the same time, for a church to make a real difference in the life of a community, it must also offer something different than simply a mirroring of the community's values. The church must have a sense of purpose and good news that comes from God, enabling it to lead constructively in the renewal of people's lives. The church must truly believe that it has something to offer that the world cannot live without![10]

Because the congregation is a disciple-forming community, this focus on mission is often lived out not through all-church projects but rather through the involvement of those who have the passion and gifts for a particular type of ministry. This means that there need not be a vote on every ministry in the community that is undertaken. Rather, those who have the passion and the gifts should be encouraged to simply do it! We'll look further at this issue when we consider lean, permission-giving structures. For now, however, it is important to note that the focus on mission is most effectively realized when people are set free to minister. The church's corporate commitment to mission is lived out, not in corporate action, but through the ministry of the disciples it is forming.

The challenges that follow from a focus on mission are many. But a congregation that has a reawakened sense of being part of God's mission in the world will acquire riches beyond measure—in the children who learn for the first time that someone really loves them, in the adults who experience in new ways the power of Jesus Christ to transform their lives and bring new meaning and possibilities to them, in their own joy from sharing God's love with others and receiving it back in unsuspected and overwhelming ways.

GIFTS AND CALL AS THE BASIS FOR MINISTRY

The driving force for ministry in the disciple-forming congregation is finding the specific, personal places where each person can faithfully and joyfully meet the needs of the world with the love of Jesus Christ. This means discovering the gifts that God has given and discerning the ways to use those gifts in responding to a call from God to ministry in Christ's name.[11]

Anyone who has ever served on a church nominating committee knows the problems involved in filling slots on an organizational chart. While you usually don't have to resort to arm-twisting and threats, the process can often involve a good measure of pleading and some measure of guilt production. Sadly, that's the way it often is when our focus is on position rather than ministry, on responsibilities rather than gifts, on recruitment rather than call.

In all too many churches the New Testament teaching about gifts hasn't yet moved off the pages of the Bible and begun to shape the life of the community. We think about proper procedures to be followed rather than gifts to be developed. We think about slots on boards to be filled rather than gifts to be celebrated and used. And too often even if gifts are considered, the central concern is how they might be used in church roles rather than how can they be used for ministry in the world. We tend to make accountants treasurers, carpenters trustees, and put women in charge of the kitchen, rather than help them discern the gifts and call that are uniquely theirs.

Two biblical insights into gifts have profound meaning for the ministry of the congregation. First, all believers are gifted—each one has been endowed by God with a gift to be used in ministry.[12] Second, God provides abundant resources, including gifts, for the ministry of the community of faith. If the ministry truly is God's, then the gifts that are needed to perform it will be available.[13] These insights are articles of faith in disciple-forming congregations.

Both of these insights lead the disciple-forming congregation to place a significant emphasis on discerning gifts. This is the work of a community, for gifts need other people to see them, name them, and call them forth. True God-given gifts are often so much a part of who we are that we are not aware of them as anything special, thinking they are pretty ordinary qualities that just about everyone must have. It is in the setting of a community of faith where we are known and where we trust others enough to listen deeply to them that we can begin to discover our gifts. This same setting is needed as we begin to use those gifts, for it provides the acceptance and affirmation that are essential to risking new behaviors.

Much the same can be said of call. God's call does come to the individual, but in most cases it takes the community of faith to make it real. The community can be the voice of God, issuing the call. The community can be that place in which the call is tested to insure that it is valid. The community can provide the support that is essential to living out the call. God often calls individuals to difficult places and risky situations. Without the support of the community of faith, living out the call may be impossible. The congregation is important to call, even if the call is not to ministry within the congregation itself. To turn people loose for ministry in the world is not to lose them. It is, rather, the living out of God's vision for the church as a sender of disciples into the world.

A concern for institutional functioning has often had the effect of directing people exclusively to roles within the congregational structure. Many gift discovery processes in fact do just that by indicating typical church responsibilities that can be fulfilled by people with particular gifts, while totally ignoring ways those gifts might be used in ministry in the world. As this institutionally focused pattern gives way to a fuller understanding of our involvement in God's mission, the congregation will need to find new ways of discernment, encouragement, and support.

SHARED MINISTRY OF LAITY AND CLERGY

The disciple-forming congregation lives out the belief that God calls both laity and clergy. Ministry, both within the church and in the world, is shared. Pastoral care happens through a variety of relationships and structures. Leadership is based on the gifts and skills of those involved.

When gifts and call become the basis for ministry, our whole understanding of who does what in the church changes—particularly the understanding we have of the roles of clergy and laity. If gifts and call are the basis for ministry, the distinctions based upon those roles change. It may even be that some congregations will discover there is no longer any basis for those distinctions. Those gifted and called to pastoral care handle that ministry within the congregation. Those gifted and called to administration handle that ministry. Those gifted and called to evangelism handle that ministry.

All of this means that the traditional distinctions between clergy and laity become less obvious as the congregation discovers the true meaning of ministry of the laity. There is a growing sense today of the need to redefine the relationship that exists between clergy and laity. The essence of the critique is that laity have been reduced to those responsible for the maintenance and supervision of the institution, while clergy are those hired to perform ministry: "The most fundamental task of lay leadership . . . is to raise money, in order to pay somebody else to do ministry and mission."[14] Once hired, the staff of the church carries the responsibility for the pastoral care of those who hired them and for doing ministry on their behalf. These "hired hands" are the ministers of the congregation. Carlyle Marney was one of the first to raise this issue for contemporary Christians. In *Priests to Each Other,* published in 1974, he described the emerging revolution in the church, noting that it would be driven by "a still unexploited insight of the great Martin Luther. The 'priest at every elbow' means that we are 'priests to each other,' the 'priesthood of every believer.'"[15] The recovery of the priesthood of believers would, in Marney's thinking, make for profound changes in the church and its relationship with the world:

> The [laity] must become the ministry of the church in the world. It is yours! This forces us to redefine everything! It is not that you as [laity] are to pitch in and help out; it's that you are the only hope we have and this forces us to redefine everything! . . . The aim of the church is not to enlist its [laity] in its services; the aim is to put [laity] as theological competents in the service of the world![16]

Pastoral care is the area in which most congregations will have the first, and perhaps greatest, struggle with this new understanding of shared ministry. It is an almost universal assumption that the pastor will be the primary caregiver of the church. Sometimes this assumption is so deeply embedded it is not even articulated. It is just expected that this is the only way it can or should be. When a church member is in the hospital, it is expected that the pastor will visit regularly. Other expected pastoral duties typically include visitation of the homebound members, counseling, as well as sensitivity to special situations that need attention. If these are not attended to there can be significant negative repercussions. Pastors themselves know that even if they are committed to significant change in a church, the primary means of gaining the credibility to fuel that change is careful attention to pastoral care.

If, however, we are committed to a significant ministry of the laity based in gifts and call, pastoral care will be seen in a different light. Are there those in the congregation other than the pastor who have this gift and call? Might there actually be others who are more gifted in this area than the pastor? Is it fair to deny them the living out of their call because of some predetermined assumptions based in role? Is it fair to demand expertise from the pastor in an area of ministry that may not be her or his gift? Might there in fact be other areas of ministry for which the pastor is more gifted and to which the pastor should devote more attention?

Congregations that have a commitment to becoming disciple-forming communities have a special obligation to consider their assumptions about pastoral care as a shared ministry of clergy and laity. If they cannot and continue to insist that the pastor play the role of primary caregiver in the church, irrespective of gifts, then their desire is not for a pastor, but for a chaplain. Chaplains do good and important work, but their gifts are not the same as those needed by leaders in a disciple-forming community.

This is a sensitive and important issue and one that challenges deeply embedded assumptions about the role of the pastor. The challenge I personally experienced in this came as I began to redirect my efforts into other areas of ministry and therefore spent less time in the traditional pastoral care activities that the congregation had come to expect. The previous pastor, for example, visited all the homebound members of the congregation each month, but I did not. This led a number of people in the congregation to conclude that I wasn't doing my job. We continued to work on this concern and the reasons for my different approach to my pastoral responsibilities, but there were still those who found this difficult to accept and who continued to interpret it as a sign that I did not care about people. Needless to say, this was not something I found easy to hear being said about myself!

As the concern continued, I became aware of a number of conflicting attitudes at work in me. First, I had to contend with my own sense of myself as a pastor. The message I was receiving seemed to be saying, "If you were a good pastor you would be doing this." If I continued in this different approach to pastoral leadership how would I confirm for others and myself that I really was a good pastor? Second, I had to deal with a genuine concern for the people who had obvious needs that were no longer being met in ways they once had been. It was out of that concern that the need to nurture laity in pastoral care became clear. This was the way in which the needs of others could still be addressed while I redirected my efforts. Third, I had to accept the "loss of status" that no longer being the primary caregiver for the congregation brought. I would no longer be the one privy to the details of everyone's life concerns. I would no longer be the one people turned to first when a pastoral care need developed. The challenge for me became one of my own ego, my own source of strength, worth, and well-being.

The living out of this shared ministry does not stop with pastoral care. It relates to every aspect of the ministry of the church, both within and outside. It insists that laity do more than manage the organization and its staff, but become the primary ministers of the church, taking their ministry into the world as they serve in Christ's name. It requires that clergy give up any automatic assumptions of role, any automatic privilege based in role. It requires that clergy minister out of their own gifts and urge laity to do the same.

A COMMITMENT TO EQUIPPING

Equipping is the work of preparation. When gifts are discovered and a call is discerned, skills and knowledge are needed in order for ministry to be faithful and effective. A disciple-forming congregation mobilizes its resources to insure that this equipping takes place. It provides opportunities to learn about the faith, as well as to develop the skills that are needed for ministry. It encourages and supports those who seek this preparation, both through opportunities offered by the church and those found elsewhere.[17]

When the ministry is shared because ministry of the laity is taken seriously, when gifts and call are the basis for ministry, then a deep commitment to equipping is essential. As we discovered in an earlier chapter, this kind of equipping involves attention to gifts and call, as well as skills and knowledge. We looked more deeply at gifts and call in a previous section. Our focus here will be on the ways in which the congregation provides the skills and knowledge needed for faithful discipleship.

There was a time when the Sunday school was the primary training and equipping vehicle of the church. It no longer is. And for good reason. The equipping that is needed for discipleship in today's world is far more extensive, far more diverse than any Sunday school could provide. There is certainly still a place for the Bible study and life issue discussion that Sunday school provides, but that alone cannot equip disciples. Many congregations recognized this long ago and began sending "leaders" to training events and workshops. There they were equipped to fulfill their leadership roles within the church. But today even more is needed.

The disciple-forming congregation honors the call of all its members and takes seriously its role in equipping them. If the congregation's focus is on God's mission lived out in a shared ministry determined by gifts and call, then a whole new kind of equipping is needed. Learning how to play roles within the institution is now a secondary concern; learning to minister in the world is primary. Because the places of ministry are as diverse as the calls that come from God, the congregation needs to provide a great variety of equipping opportunities. It can no longer continue to think about providing these opportunities itself or even through the training that is available from the denomination or para-church organizations. Where will the person whose call is to work with at-risk youth be equipped? What about the person who wants to provide a support group for caregivers? Or those who want to address the issues of poverty?

The time has come for congregations to radically rethink their role as equippers for ministry. If the skills and knowledge that people need for ministry can be found in courses in a community college, the congregation should turn there. If the congregation is serious about equipping people for ministry, it will also need to consider how it will provide the financial support that makes taking these courses possible. Some training can continue to come in traditional ways, through church-oriented events, but more and more the disciple-forming congregation will need to look elsewhere to equip members for the ministries to which they have been called.

Clearly this has budget implications. In most churches the continuing education budget is quite small and used almost exclusively for clergy and for training people for leadership roles within the church. In the disciple-forming congregation the "equipping" budget will be a high priority and used primarily by laity who are being equipped for ministry outside the church. The change is a significant one, but the disciple-forming congregation recognizes that it cannot encourage people to use their gifts in the ministry to which God has called them without also providing the essential support that will help insure their ministry will be effective. It is all part of what it means to form disciples.

LEAN, PERMISSION-GIVING STRUCTURES

Disciple-forming congregations minimize their operational structure in order to maximize their mission involvement. They discern the values and visions God has for them, making certain all their ministers know what they are. Then they allow people to do what God calls them to do. The number of positions needed to maintain the institution is minimal. People no longer need to go through a bureaucratic process of seeking permission to do mission. The congregation relies upon mutual trust and accountability based in a clearly understood purpose for ministry.

Most churches are overly structured. Their organizational structures were developed with a concern for institutional maintenance, not mission. They are based in a belief in a hierarchy through which order and control is maintained and everyone knows what is going on, if they are not actually involved in the decision that is made. There is a board or committee for everything and everything has its appropriate board or committee. And there is a coordinating council. And many decisions are made by the congregation as a whole. If there is any uncertainty about jurisdiction, issues will be considered by however many boards or committees might have possible responsibility before they are considered by the executive committee and possibly the entire congregation. That kind of structure requires a lot of people and a lot of meetings. It almost always insures that little or no ministry will happen.

Shortly after he began serving on the board of deacons, a new and younger member of a church helped organize a group of men that decided to play golf together. He showed up at the golf club at the appointed time, golf shoes on and clubs in hand only to be greeted by stares of wonder and disbelief. When he explained he was there to play golf he was informed that he was confused—this was the meeting to talk about playing golf!

The structure that is typical in most churches undercuts ministry because it requires great amounts of time, energy, and talent. Once the needs of the structure are served, there is little left for actual ministry. Capable and gifted people who might respond to a call to ministry in God's world are exhausted from institutional maintenance. Or, at the very least, their involvement in the church's institutional structure means they simply do not have the time to consider where God might be calling them to involvement in the world. This structure further undercuts ministry because its process of redundant decision-making often makes it exceedingly difficult to gain the necessary agreement to proceed, even when a person has a deep sense of call. Ministry, by its very nature, is often risky and controversial. A decision-making process that requires broad agreement does not encourage risk or controversy. In fact, one of its most cherished purposes is to ensure that there will be little of either.

Even more than this, however, this kind of organizational structure does not serve the disciple-forming congregation well because it does not respond to the needs of the people who are called upon to maintain it. It requires long-term commitment to broad areas of concern, when most people today are seeking short-term commitments to specific challenges. It requires coordinated planning that leads to the recruitment of people to implement already-determined plans, when most people today want to plan their own style of involvement. Jeff Woods refers to this as a desire for primary rather than secondary planning, a desire that is not met by traditional congregational structures. "Churches are shifting from an institutional type of planning process to a more passionate planning process . . . . Primary planning involves putting together a team that has a vested or primal interest in the topic."[18] In most cases this "primal interest" will be based in gifts and call, and it will bring with it a high level of commitment. But this can only work if the congregation is willing to turn this group loose to plan and do as it will.

The structure of a disciple-forming congregation is lean. It has the bare minimum of groups and people on them that is needed to maintain the organization. Lawrence Richards and Clyde Hoeldtke have pointed out that this is not just the practical way to organize a church; it is the biblical way. Drawing a distinction between an organism and an enterprise, they advocate an understanding of the church as an organism, the body of Christ. As such, they say, "The first priority of the organism must always be the nurture, growth, and maturity of itself and its members. The first priority of an enterprise must always be the successful achievement of its task objectives."[19] In their view permanent structures should be limited only to those enterprise functions that are "tasks absolutely necessary for the body to gather as an organism."[20] All other functions of the church are ministries to be carried out by those who are gifted and called to fulfill them. This means, in their view, that the Sunday school, for example, is not supported by a permanent board of the church but by persons who are gifted and called to that particular ministry.

In a similar vein Tom Bandy maintains that the permanent groups in a congregation should be limited to those that insure its core values and beliefs and enhance its ability to engage people in ministry. He proposes that in addition to an official board that is concerned only for the ongoing encouragement of the church's mission, the congregation have only three permanent groups: a human resources team to aid the process of discerning gifts and call; a training team to envision, train, and motivate for ministry; and an administration team, to mobilize the assets of the congregation to support people in the ministries to which they have been called. All other groups in the church are ministry teams made up of those who share a passion to respond to a particular need in the congregation or community.[21]

The structure of a disciple-forming congregation is also permission giving. It is oriented to action, not discussion. It has a bias to saying "yes" to ministry rather than "no" or "wait and see." Bill Easum describes the organization of a permission-giving church this way:

> The purpose of organization in permission-giving churches is to provide the environment in which individuals live out their spiritual gifts in the everyday world and pass on to others what they are learning about the application of their spiritual gifts to daily living. If a church emphasizes spiritual gifts, it is essential that it also gives permission for everyone to use his or her spiritual gifts.[22]

This does not mean a chaotic mess in which everyone does what he or she wishes. The boundaries are set by a clear understanding of the congregation's mission, vision, and values. Rather than spelling out power and responsibilities and seeking to control, a permission-giving structure seeks to turn people loose for any ministry opportunities that may arise within those boundaries.

This approach to structure is a direct contradiction of most church constitutions. Whether the congregation has the freedom to order itself as it chooses or not, it is usually not best to begin the process of transformation by attempting to change the structure. My approach has always been to simply encourage people to do what they believe they are called to do. Thus, for example, when a church member shared his frustration at the slowness of receiving approval for a new men's group, I encouraged him to simply share his hopes for such a group with the congregation and invite those who were interested to join him. This resulted in an active small group experience that lasted for a year, after which several other groups were started, each with a different focus. This approach leads to action and is likely to produce some positive results. It might also raise questions about proper authorization and organizational accountability. If it does, it is then possible to have the discussion about structure in concrete, rather than abstract, terms. The best and most effective time to change structure is when a growth in ministry bumps up against existing structure in such a way that the need for change is evident.

Holistic Small Groups

In a disciple-forming congregation most of the spiritual and life nurture, learning, pastoral care, and ministry occurs in and through healthy small groups.

These groups come together around a variety of concerns—from Bible study, to prayer, to support, to service. All of them include prayer, sharing, learning, and ministry as a part of their life together.

The primary organizational unit of the disciple-forming congregation is the holistic small group. If a group is holistic it engages the whole person—body, mind, and spirit—in experiences of deepening, equipping, and ministering. This should not be the only place this happens; but if it doesn't happen in this setting something vital to the faithful forming of disciples is missing. The lean, permission-giving structure of the disciple-forming congregation exists so that these small groups can thrive.

The focus of these groups may vary. Some are primarily concerned with Bible study, others support, others mission. One might serve as the worship team for the congregation. Another might be for those who teach children. There are, however, essential elements that need to be included in every group's experience. Tom Bandy describes these as prayer, action, learning, and sharing.[23] Groups may focus on one of these over the others, but all groups should provide experiences in all areas. A group that gathers primarily for support also does Bible study and is concerned about how the issues they are dealing with might lead them into serving others. The foundation of the worship team's ministry in the congregation is its own life together as it shares personal concerns, studies, and joins in prayer for each other and their ministry.

Groups can be formed around any issue or purpose about which people are concerned. The intention for the group is simply stated and those who wish to participate do so. It's as simple as that!

After years of attempting without success to form a traditional women's group, one church began a significant small group for women because one person stood up in worship on Sunday and explained that she would like to be part of a group that had a particular focus during the Advent season and invited others to join her. The group met during Advent and continued for an entire year of significant sharing, study, and growth in faith. Its greatest struggle was coming to an end, because even for these women there was a deeply embedded assumption that if the group ended it had failed. That is far from the truth, however. The ending of this group was reason for celebration because it was a sign of the growth that had taken place in the women who participated—growth that led them to new and different issues in their faith journeys.

In order to support the variety of small groups that is present in a disciple-forming congregation, significant experiences for training for group leaders are needed. These should include learning about basic group dynamics; developing methods for prayer, action, learning, and sharing; and significant involvement in their own small group. In fact, during the training, it might well be that the training experience itself provides the small group experience for participants. Most significantly, however, the training of group leaders will include mentoring or apprenticeship—working with an experienced leader to co-lead a small group. Through this experience the new leader has the benefit of continuing feedback as well as a more experienced leader with whom to discuss his or her own sense of leadership effectiveness.

The key to the development of these groups is to allow as much freedom as possible. The congregation sets the boundaries in its values, beliefs, and mission. These will include expectations for leadership in the group. Any group that does not violate these boundaries is encouraged and supported in its formation and ongoing life.

❖

These eight qualities are key to the ability of any congregation to be a disciple-forming community. They will appear in different ways in different congregations. Not all of them will be clearly present in every congregation. They provide, however, the essential raw material out of which a congregation will craft itself into a disciple-forming community. We turn now to the issue of the leadership that is needed in a congregation if these kinds of changes are to happen.

Seven ❖ Leadership in the Disciple-Forming Congregation

I HAVE A RECURRING VISION. IT IS OF THE CRUCIFIXION. A few people are gathered around the cross. A larger crowd stands off at a distance. In that group are people who might be considered church leaders—denominational staff, consultants, writers of books about congregational renewal. There are times I think I might be there, too. They are talking among themselves. The conversation goes something like this: "This is heartbreaking. He had so many gifts. He had so much potential. He cared so deeply, thought so profoundly, had such a vision for the way God is at work in the world. It is a tragedy it had to end this way. It's too bad he didn't come to the conflict resolution workshop we offered last month."

Whatever else this vision is about, it offers a clear message that leadership in the church is not ultimately about acquiring the latest skills. Knowing all the latest conflict resolution, vision discernment, growth producing, strategic planning, and spiritual discipline techniques is not what leadership is about. And they certainly do not guarantee success—at least in the way the world views success. They will not make you a "turnaround pastor" or your church a "turnaround church." They will not insure that you avoid conflict or even heartbreak and tragedy. You can know all of them and still get crucified. And the thing about it is, it may even be that this is precisely what God's intention was all along. Let's reflect on this a bit.

No one I know would make the claim that Jesus was not loving enough or wise enough or gifted enough or skilled enough. Jesus, as attuned to God's Spirit as he was, must have had whatever it took to be successful. And yet, he was hung on a cross. We know why that happened. We can explain the theology of it. But, if we were to apply many of the standards of leadership that are current today—ones that we apply to ourselves and other leaders in the church, we would be forced to conclude that his ministry was a failure. He got people so upset that they killed him.

Let's probe what all of this might mean for leadership in the church as I share with you about my experience in two churches. The first church grew significantly in a short period of time. Within three years of my arrival as pastor, the giving had increased 30 percent and worship attendance had increased about 20 percent. We had also hired the associate pastor the church had talked about having for twenty years. These changes were not without pain—both for the congregation and myself and, as is often the case, that pain expressed itself in conflict. After more than a year of attempting to move the church to deal positively with that conflict and finding myself increasingly consumed by it, I decided it was time for another kind of experience. I became the pastor of another, smaller church. In my six years there worship attendance declined, the struggle over budget grew, people got upset, and not a few of them blamed me. But, in my view it was a good ministry—dealing with the issues that needed to be dealt with, refusing to play the old games, loving and caring for everyone as best I could. About midway through my six-year pastorate there I received an insight that has become a key to my notion of leadership. My experience in both churches led me to the conclusion that I could never be the pastor they needed unless I was willing to lead them into the stress that we were experiencing, live with the blame that some wanted to place on me, continue to pursue God's vision, and stay with it until the time was right to move on. It was important for me to understand, however, that when I moved on, it needed to be with the recognition that if I had done my job well there was a very good chance that the next pastor would come, new and good things would begin to happen, and the people would say, "You see, the problem really was Jeff all along." Some people think that is a negative and fatalistic attitude. I think, although overstated for dramatic impact, it describes the focus and sacrifice that are required for effective and faithful leadership in the church today. It means being willing to sacrifice peace, comfort, being well-thought-of, and receiving credit in order to remain faithful to the call that God has given. I don't wish those sacrifices for myself or anyone. I don't work to bring them upon myself. But I do understand that this is something I have to accept if it comes my way. The measure of the real success I had in my two pastorates is directly related to the extent to which I was able to live out of that insight.

I'm not trying to encourage the adoption of a messianic complex. Neither do I want to hold up crucifixion as the ultimate sign of successful leadership. I do want to underscore, however, that leaders in the church are about something other than knowing the latest stuff and applying the latest skills. That can be helpful, but it cannot be the sole content of our leadership. And even more, leaders in the church are about something other than producing quantifiably successful results. We have as our model a person who was, in the words of a song I remember from long ago, "a flop at thirty-three."

One of my deepest beliefs about leadership is: the "who" of it is more important than the "what" of it. This is another way of saying that leadership is not about technique, but it pushes that statement a bit further. It contends that at the end of the day what will have had the greatest impact on our role as leaders is who we are as persons. That matters a whole lot more than the knowledge and skills of leadership we have accumulated along the way. The "who" of it is about those things we say and do when there is no time for reflection, in the unguarded moments when circumstances demand a response. It is determined by the spirit within that we have nurtured over the years. It is shaped by the knowledge and skills that are within because we have internalized them. It has its foundation in our own ability to face, change, and celebrate the persons that we are.

I believe Parker Palmer was right when he wrote:

> A leader is a person who has an unusual degree of power to create the conditions under which other people must live and move and have their being—conditions that can either be as illuminating as heaven or as shadowy as hell. A leader is a person who must take special responsibility for what's going on inside him or her self, inside his or her consciousness, lest the act of leadership create more harm than good.[1]

We need to take care that it is our light and not our shadow that is being projected on the people we lead. The who of it is more important than the what of it.

That, in a nutshell, is what Jesus' temptation in the wilderness was about. It was a time in which he faced himself honestly, struggled over his "who," and decided what he and his ministry would be about. That kind of intense self-reflection is essential to effective leadership. We can be thankful that the Christian faith has abundant resources for meeting this challenge.

THE TEMPTATIONS OF LEADERSHIP

It is easy to be tempted by leadership. Tempted by the ability to do good things. Tempted by the ego satisfaction that comes with the leader role. Tempted by the influence and status that come to us. Tempted by the chance to do things our way, when we have perhaps been critical of the way others have done things. For all of us, our motivations for leadership are mixed and often confused. The sense of call that beckons is real and the vision that motivates is worthy. But just as certainly, the attraction of power is addictive and the capacity for self-delusion is great. It is at best difficult to sort out our own ego needs from the genuine desire to serve, our love of power from our love of people, our sense of God's call from our own grandiose schemes. But also for all of us, bringing the best "who" that we are to our leadership role depends upon understanding those motivations and the way they impact what we say and do.

In *The Active Life* Parker Palmer offers a number of insights into the temptation of Jesus that provide a model for reflection for anyone in a position of leadership.[2] Basing his discussion on the account in Luke 4:1–15, Palmer identifies four temptations that confronted Jesus:

1. The temptation to prove one's self—"If you are the Son of God . . ." (v. 3a).
2. The temptation to be relevant—". . . command this stone to become a loaf of bread" (v. 3b).
3. The temptation to power—"To you I will give their glory and all this authority . . ." (v. 6.).
4. The temptation to be spectacular—". . . throw yourself down from here . . ." (v. 9).

These are temptations faced by every leader.

The temptation to prove one's self. We all have a personal investment in our role. We may believe we have earned it. Or, we may be insecure about it. Or, we may think we need to demonstrate that we deserve it. Or, we may consider every concern, issue, or problem that comes before us as a personal test of worthiness. None of these may be driving forces in our lives, but it is a good bet that some of them are there beneath the surface waiting to be hooked by a particular comment or situation. And when they are, we will sense the need to prove ourselves.

- If you really believe the Bible is the Word of God, you . . .
- If you really are committed to Jesus, you . . .
- If you really are a loyal member of this congregation, you . .
- If you really are a caring pastor, you . . .
- If you really have a commitment to justice, you . . .

How might each of these be completed in a way that tempts you to prove yourself? I've found that the temptation to prove myself can surface in a number of ways. On the one hand I sense it's working on me when people question my commitment to issues about which I feel strongly—such as racism or sexism. If others say they don't see that commitment in me I can be tempted to prove it to them in ways that may not be appropriate to me or to the situation in which I find myself. Another point of temptation for me comes in areas in which I realize I am challenging some of the traditional roles of the pastor. My commitment to disciple-forming in the congregation, for example, results, as I mentioned earlier, in my spending less time in pastoral care than many pastors. So when people question my caring for those in the congregation I can sense the pangs of uncertainty begin to intensify.

Jesus, whom the Holy Spirit had already proclaimed as God's Son (Luke 3:22), also faced this temptation to prove himself. It is a question of identity. Jesus was tempted, as we all are, but in the strength of his relationship with God he found the resources to reject the taunting of the devil. His understanding of his call, his reason for being, enabled him to withstand the temptation. That resistance, in turn, strengthened his sense of call. "Jesus does not regard himself as accountable for his calling to any voice except God's, so in his refusal to 'prove' anything to the devil he is actually proving that he is the Chosen One as he himself understands it."[3] This temptation will come to us in areas in which we do not have the confidence that comes from the strength of relationship and identity that Jesus had.

The temptation to be relevant. Jesus was hungry. That was the immediate need, the need to which the devil appealed in telling him to turn a stone into bread. But Jesus understood the big picture. He knew this was about something more than the immediate. He understood that the real issue was his call and the role he was to play in God's mission. To focus on his hunger as a problem to be solved would undercut his ability to address the deeper concern. The temptation to be relevant is the temptation to solve the problems of the moment—the budget crisis, the upset parishioner, the controversy over music—rather than stay focused on the bigger issue. Often these issues, although the demand upon us to solve them may be great, are not what matters most. And often, addressing them actually undercuts our ability to deal with the deeper concern. They can in fact be nothing more than diversionary tactics used by those who do not want the deeper concerns addressed. "Jesus' real need is for inward confirmation of his mission, a confirmation he is more likely to find in the emptiness of fasting than in the gratification of bodily needs."[4] As with Jesus, our real need is to respond to God's call—in our case, to become a disciple-forming community. The immediate, pressing, and seemingly relevant concerns that abound in a congregation can distract us and even cause us to ignore that call. I think I am probably not alone in my experience that the seemingly pressing concern to increase church membership can easily distract from attending to the deeper concerns related to becoming a disciple-forming congregation, so that those who come to the church will have a reason to stay.

The temptation to power. To be a leader is to exercise power, yet all power corrupts. This is the great dilemma every leader faces. The temptation that Jesus faced was to use his abilities to draw power to himself for himself, power over others. Having this power is, after all, the way to get things done. And if what we want to get done is God's work, it is possible to cloak a desire for this power in all sorts of pious rationalizations. Jesus cut through all of that. He realized that the power that was being offered was an illusion. "Power and glory are not the devil's to give. They belong to God alone, and only through God can we share in them."[5] To be about God's work is never to take power, no matter the temptation it offers—even the temptation to do good. It is always to share it with others. How we use the power that is granted us as leaders depends upon our own ability to live as disciples of Jesus and it determines our ability to help form others in their discipleship. We cannot do that by exercising power over them, only by empowering them.

The temptation to be spectacular. Imagine how many people would become believers if, with their own eyes, they saw God save a man falling from the tallest steeple in town! Imagine how many would come to Christ if we could only install a new video and sound system in our sanctuary or get a new pipe organ or have a beautiful colonial sanctuary! Imagine how many people would be saved if we could double the size of our church within the next year or take a mission trip every summer or have the biggest youth group in town! This is the temptation to be spectacular. It is the temptation Jesus faced when the devil challenged him to throw himself off the pinnacle of the temple. He even quoted scripture in an attempt to prove that God would always protect him! The key, of course, is the motivation behind the acts. Is it to serve our ego, to demonstrate our "success," to enhance our prestige, to make others stand in awe? Those are not easy questions to answer honestly, but doing that is essential to faithful leadership. Jesus knew. That's why he said, "Do not put the Lord your God to the test" (v. 12). And that's why the devil went away—at least for a while.

This is the temptation I experience when I hear the stories of churches that have grown significantly in just a few years or of churches that have transformed their inward focus and taken on a new passion for mission in their communities. These are great stories! But they, almost by their very nature, prime the juices of envy or competition within me. They tempt me to do things that are just as spectacular—perhaps to validate my leadership, perhaps to prove the greatness of the God we serve, perhaps to reach more people with God's love. It is easy to cloak this temptation in pious words— even the devil did that. No matter the rationale, however, it is still a temptation to be resisted.

The temptation to be inadequate. There is another side to this temptation coin, one not experienced by Jesus—at least in the Gospel accounts. It is the temptation—not to be more than we rightfully can be—but less. Palmer calls it the temptation to be inadequate. It may not be the most common temptation among those who find themselves in a leadership position, but it could very well be the temptation our congregations face. In the face of the changes and challenges that confront many congregations, there is a temptation to give up—to say we're just a small church or we don't have the money or the people or the skills we need. It is, Palmer says, "the temptation to think of ourselves as irrelevant, powerless, and utterly mundane."[6] The error of this belief is that it is based in the assumption that in order to be effective and faithful the congregation must be relevant, powerful, and spectacular! It's the same mistake we encountered in the other temptations, just in a different form. And it can do a church in. It can immobilize it, depress it, and cause it to cocoon, becoming little more than an institutional hospice. It, too, is a temptation that leaders need to acknowledge and resist—if not for themselves, then perhaps for their churches.

The Characteristics of Leadership

Aware of the temptations leaders face, we can now move on to look at some positive characteristics that are important for leaders in disciple-forming congregations. Let's begin by reminding ourselves of two characteristics of leadership that we have already affirmed.

1. In the disciple-forming community, leadership is shared by clergy and laity.[7]
2. In the disciple-forming community, leadership is based in the giftsthat God has given to each person.[8]

Because leadership in the disciple-forming congregation is a shared ministry, everything in this chapter is for both clergy and laity. Because our leadership is based in the gifts God has given, attention to the discovery and development of our own gifts is essential, as is the humility to accept what gifts we do not have and refrain from leadership that depends upon those gifts. Because gifts are essential to leadership it isn't particularly helpful to simply develop a manual that assigns specific leadership functions to specific offices—some to clergy, others to laity; some to deacons, others to trustees or elders. Rather, our purpose in this chapter is to explore leadership characteristics that underlie all roles and functions. In doing that we at least indirectly challenge traditional roles and functions. Bill Easum has encapsulated those with this insight:

> Most of today's laity function as care takers and givers rather than spiritual leaders—going to endless rounds of meaningless meetings, trying to manage and protect decaying institutions from extinction. Most of today's pastors function as chaplains—going about taking care of people, visiting shut-ins and hospitals, serving communion and mouthing archaic rituals understood by a decreasing number of people.[9]

That's not what leadership in the disciple-forming congregation is about. We won't talk about such things here.

Leadership in the disciple-forming congregation is: spiritually powered, disciple forming, vision led, servant focused, team building, and change oriented.

SPIRITUALLY POWERED

Leaders in the disciple-forming community are spiritually powered. This isn't about piety or even about praying regularly or any other spiritual discipline, although they certainly are important. Spiritually powered leadership is leadership that relies upon the Spirit to empower everything it does. The reason for this is simple: on our own we are incapable of meeting the challenge of being leaders in a disciple-forming community. Paul, in 2 Corinthians, puts it this way: "Not that we are competent of ourselves to claim anything as coming from us; our competence is from God, who has made us competent to be ministers of a new covenant . . ." (2 Corinthians 3:5–6a). It is only as we are empowered by the Spirit, only as we allow the Spirit to work in us and through us that this impossibility becomes possible. Although we are gifted and talented, lovable and capable, able to do amazing things, we are inadequate for the job that is ours. Our ability to lead both faithfully and effectively begins with our willingness to acknowledge that inadequacy—not always an easy thing for capable leaders to do. That's the only way we create room enough for the Spirit to be present.

I believe that our true effectiveness as leaders in a disciple-forming community begins with a Declaration of Incompetence. It took me a long time before I was able to stand in front of a group and say that I was incompetent. To be honest, I don't make a practice of it even today. But the ability to acknowledge this inadequacy and to talk about it publicly when appropriate has made a great difference in my ministry. It has taken away the pressure toward perfection, relieved the burden of needing to be right.

Perhaps we need to form a new group called "Competents Anonymous." It would be for all of us who are addicted to developing our competencies for the task of disciple forming. I don't mean to say by this that there are no disciple-forming skills to learn or that we shouldn't work to develop those skills. Rather, my point is that it is pure folly for us to believe that we can meet the challenge of disciple forming in this world relying on our own competencies and skills. We cannot do that because the world is changing so rapidly that today's competencies are tomorrow's curiosities, like knowing how to start a stalled car by sticking a pencil in the carburetor—my sole automotive skill. But even more, it is folly because the task of forming disciples, to say nothing of being a disciple, is humanly impossible. We simply cannot be skilled enough, competent enough, or credentialed enough to do it. Doing it depends on God and the power of God's Spirit working in us and on us and through us. As long as we think we can make it on our own, we are destined to fail. That is why the confession of our incompetence is the place we need to begin.

Are you ready to test yourself on this? Then, stop right now. Find a place you can talk out loud, maybe even shout. And say these words:

> I am incompetent.
> I do not have what it takes.
> I am incompetent.
> I do not have the skills that are needed.
> I am incompetent.
> The credentials I worked so hard to earn are not enough.
> I am incompetent.
> What little I know today won't be worth anything tomorrow.
> I am incompetent.
> If you count on me I will disappoint you.
> If it depends on me it will not happen.
> I am incompetent.

Do you feel just a bit uncomfortable saying those words? I do. Say them again. If you say them often enough you will begin to find great comfort in them. For this Declaration of Incompetence is also a Declaration of Freedom—freedom from unwarranted expectations, unbearable burdens, and impossible demands. When you find comfort in these words, you are ready to begin. Then, pray these words: "God of all knowledge, skill and power, I come to you. I confess my inability on my own to be the person you called me to be, to do the work you called me to do. I confess my incompetence. Fill me, I pray. May your power be at work within me, that

I may empower others. May your gifts flow from me, that I may give to others. May your love uplift me, that I may love others. May I open myself so completely to you that I gladly join Paul in saying, 'It is no longer I who live, but it is Christ who lives in me . . . . The life I now live in the flesh I live by faith in the Son of God, who loved me and gave himself for me.' Amen."

When we can do this (or at least acknowledge our dependence upon God in some less dramatic way!) we create room for the Spirit to be at work in us and through us. Then we can turn to the practices of spiritual discernment to help us attune ourselves to the Spirit's presence and power in our lives.

Spiritually powered leadership isn't purpose driven; it is Spirit driven. This is the art of deepening—applied to the task of leadership. The leader who forgets to discern the workings of the Spirit or neglects to nurture the spirit within will soon lose legitimate claim to leadership. The leader who continues to deepen and discern can have a profound impact on a congregation, not through his ability or her skill, but through the presence and power of the Spirit.

DISCIPLE FORMING

Leaders in the disciple-forming congregation are disciple forming. Yes, that is a redundancy, but it is also important to remember. With the onslaught of demands that every church leader faces, it is easy to forget what we are there for. This affirmation calls us back to the underlying thrust of our purpose: as leaders in the church we are there to nurture the development of a disciple-forming community. The models for being a leader in the church abound. We can be managers. We can be caregivers. We can be educators. We can be therapists. We can be marketers. We can be entertainers. We can be CEO's. We can be hospice chaplains and museum directors. The temptation to be one or another of these can be great. The pressures placed upon us by others to be one or another of these can be even greater. Those temptations must be resisted. Bill Easum had it right when he wrote: "Leaders sense that the basic genetic code of the church is to make disciples of Jesus Christ, not to take care of people"[10]—or, for that matter, to adhere to any of those other so-called models of ministry.

That is the public purpose of this redundancy, but it also has a personal purpose. It serves to remind us that as leaders we, too, are being formed as disciples. In the busyness that goes with life and leadership in the church, it may seem that there is not enough time for this. Sometimes we even rationalize the neglect of our own growth as disciples by claiming that we are so busy discipling others or doing the work of building a disciple-forming community that we have little personal time to attend to this concern. Perhaps we think we are further along the road than others and can afford to neglect our own journey for a while in order to help them. Perhaps we explain our neglect in the language of sacrifice and service to others. This is a sham! Even if it is cloaked in pious language, it is a foolish lie that neither we nor the congregation we seek to lead should tolerate.

We are being formed as disciples even as we provide leadership for the disciple-forming community. The elements of discipleship that shape that community also shape our own lives. Our concern is the ways in which deepening, equipping, and ministering are occurring in our own lives. In fact, one way in which we can take stock of our growth as disciples is to reflect periodically on our own progress. Here are questions I ask myself:

How has deepening been a part of my life these past weeks?

- In what ways have I grown in my relationship with Christ?
- In what ways have I become more aware of myself as a person—my strengths, my weaknesses, my struggles, my fears, my hopes, the temptations I face, the risks I avoid, the challenges I undertake?
- In what ways have I developed a stronger community in which to share my own faith journey and encourage the journeys of others?
- What can I do to enhance my own deepening?

How has equipping been a part of my life these past weeks?

- Have I discovered new gifts or used old ones in new ways?
- How is my call being lived out? Is it still vital? Am I sensing a new call?
- What have I learned that is important to my living as a disciple?

+ What skills have I acquired or improved that increase my ability to live as a disciple?
+ What can I do to enhance my own equipping?

How has ministering been a part of my life these past weeks?

+ In what ways is the leadership role I play my ministry?
+ In what new ways am I living out my discipleship—at home, in the church, at work, and in the community?
+ How has my involvement in ministering strengthened my life as a disciple?
+ What can I do to enhance my own ministering?

The only way we can possibly support others in their growth as disciples of Jesus Christ is to be growing disciples ourselves. It's as simple as that!

VISION LED

Leaders in the disciple-forming community are vision led. Leonard Sweet has said, "The top challenge of leadership is this: How do you get people to ask new questions, to think in different ways?"[11] That's what vision is about—helping people ask and think and see in different ways. Without a vision of the new thing God is calling us to be and do we get caught in ruts, unable to break ourselves out of old ways. Leadership in the disciple-forming congregation is led by a vision. That vision isn't theirs. It comes from God. Rarely is it the work of a committee. Even more rarely can it be put in words and posted on a wall or printed in an annual report. Certainly it needs to be shared. But that sharing is best when this happens not through pen or poster, but through the heart— maybe even, as Tom Bandy describes it, "a song in your heart."[12]

If the themes of this book have begun to resonate with you, then it's quite likely the vision that will stir you is one that relates to the congregation being a disciple-forming community. That doesn't make it as a vision, however. The vision for your congregation needs to be more specific, grow more from your own experience and life together, relate more to the setting in which you find yourself. This book can't give you the vision you need. It might be able to point a direction or sketch some possibilities in very broad strokes. But the vision itself is something you will need to seek and discern together.[13]

> A vision is not about programs and objectives or scenarios or goals. A vision is about releasing energies. A vision is about life-giving spirit. A vision is about the excitement of shared possibilities. A vision is about seeing in such a way and communicating what you see that other people come to life with new enthusiasm and resolve.[14]

SERVANT FOCUSED

Leaders in the disciple-forming community are servant focused. The intent of their leadership, both in substance and in style, is to serve others. This isn't a matter of attending to their every expressed need or fulfilling whatever demands they might have. Servanthood in the disciple-forming community is something radically different. It is based in the belief that true fulfillment comes as we discover God's intentions for us and bring them to reality in our lives—in other words, as we become disciples. The servant, then, is one who works to make that possible. The best way any of us can serve another person is to aid them in becoming the person God intended them to be. That is what leaders in the disciple-forming community do.

"The servant-leader is servant first."[15] This insight is provided by Robert Greenleaf, who from a largely secular perspective began writing in the mid-1970s about the importance of being servant focused. Drawing some on his own Quaker tradition, but writing mostly to the world of business and education, Greenleaf helped begin a conversation on servant leadership that continues to grow in importance today.

> It begins with the natural feeling that one wants to serve, to serve first. Then conscious choice brings one to aspire to lead. That person is sharply different from one who is leader first, perhaps because of the need to assuage an unusual power drive or to acquire material possessions. For such it will be a later choice to

serve—after leadership is established. The leader-first and the servant-first are two extreme types. Between them there are shadings and blends that are part of the infinite variety of human nature. The difference manifests itself in the care taken by the servant-first to make sure that other people's highest priority needs are being served.[16]

Along the way in this discussion that Greenleaf began, religious leaders discovered how essential this understanding of leadership is to the church. It was Jesus, after all, who first talked about the need for leaders to be servants of all (Mark 9:35). But what does this term servant leadership mean, really?

It means first of all that we enter into any leadership position with great humility. We are not there to have our own needs met. Some lead because it feels good to exercise power. Others lead because it feels good to help others. Both miss the point of servant leadership. To be a servant is to empty one's self, so that motivations are not based in personal ego satisfaction, but in the potential growth of others. But let's be clear. This is not about becoming a doormat or being so self-deprecating and self-sacrificing that we do injury to ourselves and our own well-being. Sometimes sacrifice is needed, but it always comes from our strength, not our weakness—from our ability to say yes, not our inability to say no.

Secondly, servant leadership is always noncoercive. People cannot be pushed or manipulated into being the persons God intends for them to be. They must go there of their own free choice. God allows that freedom. So does the leader in the disciple-forming congregation. The leadership role is one of consistently talking about potential and offering possibilities, of encouraging people to discover their own potentials and possibilities. It doesn't include the use of pressure, guilt, or even unrealistic promises of joy and fulfillment in order to tempt, force, or cajole them into making a decision they are not yet ready to make.

Thirdly, because God's intentions for us are always more than we can imagine, the servant leader focuses more on the big picture than the little details. The details are important, of course, but the context in which they fit needs always to be remembered. It is not just a decision about teaching a Sunday school class, or taking a job in another city, or getting married. As important as all of these are, their true import can only be recognized when the decisions related to them are seen in the context of God's call to be disciples and in that way fulfill God's intentions for us. Leonard Sweet says it well: "Postmodern leaders are not customer-centric but Christo-centric. Their focus is not 'what the customer wants,' but 'what Christ wants.' They look to Christ themselves, to help others find Christ in their own lives, to help the word made flesh be made fresh again."[17]

Finally, because God's call always leads us into a new future, the servant leader is more concerned about what will be than about was or even what is. Foresight is essential to the servant leader—the ability to look ahead and sense the possibilities of the future. This is true for the servant leader's role in relationship to individuals, encouraging people into the future that God intends for them. It is also true in relationship to the congregation. To see what the church will need to be two or five or ten years from now in order to fulfill its call as a disciple-forming community is one of the most significant contributions leadership can make.

Robert Greenleaf was the first person to awaken me to the challenges of leadership in my own life. In a letter to me, written over 20 years ago, he shared an insight that continues to both encourage and challenge me in my role as a servant leader in a congregation.

> The important thing for the aware individual is to function consistently as a servant, to seek to be influential, and not to destroy one's effectiveness by pushing a situation faster than it will move. This calls for a distinction between a leader and a prophet. An effective leader is pulling, but not so hard as to break the tie. The leader is always connected to what one is leading. The prophet is the far out visionary—terribly useful but usually disconnected, and therefore not leading. It seems to me that one must consciously choose which role to take because it is the rare prophet who is able to lead.

To be a servant leader is always to remain connected, to never break the ties that bind our hearts and lives in Christ and to those we are leading.

TEAM BUILDING

Leaders in the disciple-forming community are team building. Teams are essential to the disciple-forming community for two reasons.

The first reason is community. The larger community of the congregation has its foundation in the smaller communities of teams. Without teams in which people can share themselves, study together, and engage in ministry, the growth of the congregation is severely limited. If everyone needs to know and share and learn and minister with the whole congregation, growth stops once individuals have reached the limit on the number of people they can know well. Where teams are present and when there is a process of consistently adding new teams, growth can continue. Even apart from the advantages for growth, however, the community of teams is essential to disciple forming. The depth of engagement that is needed to form disciples happens best in a small group, not a large one. That group may be as small as three, but it shouldn't be any larger than twelve. That kind of group provides the best setting for deepening, equipping, and ministering. Certainly involvement in other settings is needed as well—such as worship with the congregation—but without significant involvement in a team of people committed to deepening, equipping, and ministering, growth as disciples is virtually impossible.

The second reason teams are essential is ministry. The gifts that God has given are varied. They are distributed among all disciples. No one has them all. That means that effective ministry depends upon teams in which the gifts of many are brought together "for the work of ministry" (Ephesians 4:12). The team shares a common call to ministry in a specific setting or with a specific audience. It then mobilizes the gifts of it members in order to make effective ministry possible.

Ephesians 4 indicates that these two purposes—community and ministry—are interconnected. As we noted earlier, this passage talks about "the work of ministry." That phrase is followed directly by another one: "for building up the body of Christ." They are two sides of the same coin. It is as gifts are shared in ministry that the body of Christ is made strong. The community brings together the gifts that are needed for ministry. The result of ministry is the strengthening of the community.

In the disciple-forming congregation, teams are given the freedom to be what they need to be. They spring up around common concerns, needs, and passions. They function in order to respond to those needs. They end when their members have grown in ways that lead them into new involvements. The congregation supports these teams through the training of leaders and the establishment of core practices that shape their functioning.[18]

Teams are not always easy to develop in a congregation. They require a different understanding of the way in which people work together—one in which responsibility and authority are shared. They require an openness that enables sharing with each other on a personal level, rather than just attending to the "business" of the church. In order for teams to function effectively they must have the authority to act. This is sometimes difficult to achieve in structures in which governing boards seek to maintain control over all that happens within the congregation. A different way of thinking about organization and a different set of skills are both needed if teams are to be effective.

The leadership of the disciple-forming congregation provides the model for teams in its own functioning. Leaders are not functionaries performing predetermined tasks. They are disciples who continue their own formation through participation in a team that encourages deepening, equipping, and ministering. It is a team of people called to ministry that provides the worship experiences of the congregation. It is a team of people called to ministry that provides the congregation's ministry with children. It is a team that runs the thrift shop or the soup kitchen or that organizes the community to provide positive experiences for youth or address concerns about the criminal justice system. It is always a team that does it.

CHANGE ORIENTED

Leaders in the disciple-forming community are change-oriented. They have, in the words of Bill Easum, a "holy discontent with the status quo."[19] The reason for this is simple. Although God loves us just as we are, God also always invites us to be more than we are right now. Our response to God's call, both as individuals and as a congregation, is never complete. There is always more that we can be and do—always something more wondrous that God has in store for us. That means that as disciples we are always growing, always changing. That growth and change is, of course, based in what has gone before, but it is always evolving into a new thing.

For the disciple and the disciple-forming congregation this is reason for both challenge and hope. The challenge comes as we strive to live ever more faithfully to God's call to us. The hope comes in knowing that God's purpose in creation—the purpose that is the basis of our call—will be fulfilled. Both are important to us. Challenge without hope easily leads to a sense of inadequacy, failure, and even despair. Hope without challenge easily disintegrates into laziness, leaving it all to God to work out in God's own time.

Ronald Heifetz, in *Leadership Without Easy Answers,* offers a number of insights about the reality of the change that is needed in the church. Although writing to a secular audience, his comments have great validity for congregations. Heifetz distinguishes between technical and adaptive responses to concerns, problems, and issues faced by an organization. Technical responses rely on the application of what we or an expert we hire already knows in order to solve the problems we may be experiencing. This type of change worked well for congregations in the past. It meant finding a new curriculum to improve the Sunday school or adopting a new planning process to enhance overall church programming or hiring a more skilled choir director to improve the quality of worship. Adaptive responses, on the other hand, are based in the discovery of answers that are not already known. These are the responses that are needed in today's congregation. Because the world has changed so much, the issue now isn't just improving Sunday school but discovering more effective ways to equip disciples; it isn't just planning more effective programs but becoming a community in which the practices of the faith are lived out all the time; it isn't just improving worship but engaging our culture and tradition to discover a whole new way to worship. The old answers don't work anymore, but the new ones are not yet clear. The challenge for us is to develop new responses that allow us to adapt to the new realities we face. If we cannot do this we begin to die.

Heifetz suggests that to find the adaptive responses to the challenges we face we need to learn to live with conflict. The answers we seek, he believes, are to be found in the "conflicts in the values people hold [and] the gap between the values people stand for and the reality they face."[20] Both these types of conflicts exist in most congregations. There is a difference of opinion among members over what the church should be and do. More importantly, however, there is a gap between what we profess the church to be and the reality of what it is. This is a gap between "an accurate perception of reality and God's ideal."[21] By engaging these conflicts we discover the responses that allow us to adapt to new realities so that we can live more faithfully.

Change always means conflict. The leader who is change oriented will need to be able to manage conflict as well. Heifetz suggests several important principles for doing this:

1. Identify the key challenge for your congregation, seeing every issue from the perspective of the bigger picture. The key adaptive change for any congregation will come as it answers the question: what is God calling us to be and do in this time and place?

2. Utilize the stress that conflict brings to promote change, but work to keep that stress within manageable levels. This requires a sense for how much change can be undertaken at one time.

3. Maintain the focus on the key challenge, even though there may be significant distractions in the form of avoidance, scapegoating, or attacking a perceived "enemy" who is assumed to be the cause of the problem.

4. Give the work back to the people so that they will become part of the solution. The leadership task isn't to provide answers but to help the congregation discern the answers God is providing.

5. Seek out and protect the voices of those without authority. The answers that are needed in the church today will come from the edges—from those only marginally involved, from youth, from those who are the "minorities" in your setting. These are the people in the margin, for whom the church

has lost a good bit of its meaning. When they are heard, understood, and engaged it will be possible to discover new meanings. So a task of leadership is to insure that those in the margins are recognized and heard.[22]

The process of change can be difficult. It will create conflict. With typical forthrightness, Bill Easum points out that one of the reasons for this conflict is that "most dying churches have a hand-ful of people who need to be kicked in the butt."[23] While some might consider this metaphorical suggestion a harsh judgment, it does reflect the reality in many churches and asks us to assess the situation we face honestly. Sometimes the process of change will require some butt-kicking! Even this can be done with attention to the greater claims of the gospel—not just what it calls the church to be, but also how it calls us to treat each other.

More significant, however, is the insight provided by Jim Herrington, Mike Bonem, and James Furr in their book *Leading Congregational Change*.

> The change process, by its very nature, creates conflict. A congre-gation with a high level of spiritual and relational vitality can accept change and can manage conflict in ways that gives life. Conversely, a congregation with a low level of spiritual and rela-tional vitality will tend to manage conflict in ways that preserves the status quo.[24]

This is the key to undertaking the changes that are needed to become a disciple-forming congregation. It is why spiritual vitality is the first of the qualities of a disciple-forming congregation. It is why spiritually powered is the first of the characteristics of leader-ship. It is only the Spirit's presence and power at work in us and in our congregations that makes us disciples and disciple-forming communities. That's more than a theological concept. It's the prac-tical reality of how the needed change happens.

I know all this. I believe it. And yet I still find it difficult be-cause I am not one who relishes conflict. In fact, I do not like it at all. I want people to like me. I don't want people to be angry, either with me or with each other. My stomach has an innate sense of conflict possibilities and will invariably let me know when one appears on the horizon. It is always a challenge for me to be a change-oriented leader, because I know change means conflict and I don't like conflict. I can be that kind of leader, however, because something more important is at stake. At the grand, theological level, the more important thing is God's vision for the church, God's mission for the redemption of all creation. But that something more important has a much more personal side, as well—a side that speaks to us in ways no theology ever could. You have your stories about that personal side, I'm sure. Here is one of mine.

When my older son graduated from college he went to China for a year to teach English and to enhance his fluency in Chinese. He returned home at the end of that year and spent a few weeks with us before he headed off to graduate school. The first Sunday he was home he went to church with us. The service that week was fairly typical; much like any Protestant worship service you could attend almost anywhere. I could tell from his posture and expression, however, that it was not a profound spiritual experience for him. On the way home I asked him about it and he said that he had been thinking about the church and its purpose during the service. He then asked me this question: "Why do you come every week and give all that money to support that crap when there is so much real need in the world?" In all honesty, I found that a very difficult question to answer in a way that would mean anything to him. He wasn't attacking the quality of the sermon or the music or questioning the sincerity of the people who led the service. He was, however, making a bold statement of the church's inability to share the gospel in a way that could speak directly to him and his life concerns—and to the countless other people who aren't ever present in worship. These are the people I think about when I am confronted with my dislike of conflict. If in order to reach them the church must change, if in order to change the church must engage in conflict, how can I let my own personal dislike for conflict stand in the way? It's not just about theology; it is about real people and their real lives.

❖

These characteristics of leadership in the disciple-forming congregation provide a beginning framework to both plan and assess our work as leaders. They provide the hooks upon which we can hang our insights and reflections about our own leadership, as well as our successes and failures as leaders. In that way they can be helpful. Because, as noted earlier, the "who" of leadership is more important than the "what" of leadership, what matters most is that we continue to attend to our own growth as disciples. If we are better disciples, we will be better leaders. If we are more open to God's leading in our own lives, we will be better able to lead others. This is the source from which all our leadership ability comes.

Now that we have considered both the temptations and characteristics of leadership we are ready to turn to the tasks of leadership. In the next chapter we will consider a number of different points at which it might be possible to enter the process of becoming a disciple-forming congregation.

Eight ❖ Entry Points

Up TO THIS POINT ON OUR JOURNEY OUR PRIMARY concern has been to gain an understanding of discipleship and of the qualities of disciple-forming congregations. Both of these provide a different way of looking at the life of a congregation—a way that speaks directly to the realities of the post-Christendom, postmodern world in which we live. They are important concepts to have in mind because they provide a framework for considering the ministry to which God has called us. Even without the framework, however, disciple forming goes on in most congregations. It's in the blood, so it happens even if we are not clear about what we are doing. The framework helps us gain clarity, which means we can look more clearly at what is already happening and think more clearly about what we want to happen. And, most importantly, we can actually do those things that will enhance our disciple-forming ability.

Doing that is what this chapter is about. If you have been grabbed by the concepts of discipleship and the congregation as a disciple-forming community we have talked about, you're probably ready to get to work making them a reality in your church.

There are any number of ways you can do that. That's good because it lets you pick the way that you think will work best in your situation. It's also somewhat problematic, because it means there is no pre-determined process for you to follow, no six-step plan for you to implement. You'll need to make the decision about how to proceed on your own. In the spirit of a guidebook, however, we will provide some suggestions and enough information about them for you to make an informed decision about the route you want to follow.

Because there are a great number of possible entry points, we'll organize them according to the people you would want to join you in doing them. We'll look first at things to do on your own, then things to do with kindred spirits, things to do with boards and committees, and finally, things to do with the entire congregation.

Things to Do on Your Own

The challenges of leadership in the disciple-forming community are great. We looked at a number of those in the last chapter. Here our concern will be those things you as a leader can do to prepare yourself to encourage the movement of your congregation toward being a disciple-forming community.

Look at ways in which you are deepening, equipping, and ministering. Your own continuing growth as a disciple is essential to your ability to participate effectively in the development of a disciple-forming community. Appendix A offers questions for your reflection that will help you assess areas of strength and weakness in your ongoing growth. Once you have answered the questions, make plans to become more active in areas in which you have not done much recently.

Strengthen your own spiritual life. This, of course, is one of the dimensions of deepening, but it is of such critical importance that it needs to be mentioned separately. Appendix C offers one way in which to do that. Use the descriptors of a disciple of Jesus to prayerfully reflect upon each of these dimensions of your relationship with him. Don't rush through this. You may want to use a devotional time each day to consider each dimension separately. Beyond this there are many resources you can use for your own personal spiritual growth. Many of these provide daily experiences for reflection. It is not necessary to be restricted to daily experiences, however. It may be that weekly or some other longer timeframe works more effectively for you. One of the most significant experiences I have had occurred only when I traveled. I would select a book of the Bible to read during the trip. I would read it, then read it again—as many times as I could on the trip. This repetition led to the realization that certain phrases or verses began to speak more clearly to me than others, which then led to more focused meditation on those passages in order to understand what God was saying to me in them.

Read about congregational change and transformation. It is important for you to begin to learn more about the process of transformation and change in congregations. This book approached that from the distinct perspective of becoming a disciple-forming community. Others offer different perspectives, but many are compatible and all of them provide helpful insights that you can use in your congregation. The books listed in appendix 6 provide a good beginning point for your reading.

Begin to adjust your own behavior. One of the ways institutions change is for some people to no longer participate in the old ways of doing things or to start to do new things. This disrupts the system and can create tension, but people do take notice and it can be the beginning point for significant change. You might want to think about things you will not do anymore and/or other things you will begin to do. Here are some possibilities, but the list is endless. They are simple things really.

1. Just say no! If you are tired of going to board and committee meetings that seem to accomplish little but continue to do so out of a sense of obligation, then say "No" the next time someone on the Nominating Committee asks you to serve in a particular office.
2. Just go! Begin to consider the specific gifts that God has given you and find ways to use them—not necessarily in the church, but in ministry in the community.
3. Just do it! Whenever you are in a position to give permission, do so. Don't wait for the next board meeting to make

certain everyone agrees. Or, if there is something you would like to do in the way of forming a group or engaging in ministry simply ask if anyone has the same interest and would like to join you. Avoid the lengthy, and often debilitating, process of seeking permission.

4. Just change! If you are the pastor, begin to adjust your own involvements to reflect the priorities of the disciple-forming church. Spend less time on pastoral care and more on equipping others. Spend less time maintaining structure and more time helping people discern their gifts. Spend less time preparing the sermon alone and more time preparing worship with others. Spend less time as a teacher and more time as a spiritual guide. All of these are important aspects of the role the pastor plays in the congregation. In all likelihood none of them involves an either/or decision. In fact, they sometimes complement each other. It is, however, a matter of priorities. The shift to becoming a disciple-forming community involves a change in priorities of the pastor.

5. Just share your own need! Talk about being a disciple and how you would like more support from the congregation in your own efforts to follow Jesus more fully.

6. Just stop! Refuse to let yourself be sucked into doing things in the church out of a sense of duty or because no one else will or because it will otherwise mean the end of a longstanding program or ministry. Refuse to bemoan the lack of leaders needed for programs. The lack of willing leaders may well be God's way of saying it's time to call it quits on this one.

THINGS TO DO WITH KINDRED SPIRITS

Many of the suggestions from the previous section can be done with kindred spirits. Kindred spirits are the people you don't have to explain things to. They resonate with the concerns and hopes you have for your church. You don't have to convince them of anything. They just seem to "get it." Perhaps you gave them a copy of this book and they got excited about it. Or perhaps it's the person who gave you this book to read. You know who they are because conversations with them about issues that concern you give you a positive sense that someone else does understand. The suggestions here are geared mainly to kindred spirits in your own congregation. But you may very well find them elsewhere. If you do, find ways to connect and share with them. Kindred spirits are an important source of support and encouragement no matter where they are found.

Kindred spirits are essential partners with you in your own growth as a disciple through deepening, equipping, and ministering. They can provide fresh perspectives and new insights that enhance your growth.

Kindred spirits are a great support in strengthening your spiritual life. Perhaps you will want to meet regularly or go on periodic retreats together. You might use the same resource for a time so that you can share about your experience with each other.

Kindred spirits enrich your experience of reading about congregational change and transformation. If you are reading the same book at the same time you can share your reactions and consider their meaning for your church together.

Kindred spirits join you as you begin to adjust behavior. Two or three people doing this will have a greater impact on the congregation. If others in the congregation see and hear more than one person making these adjustments, they are more likely to take notice. It may intensify the stress, but it can also make movement toward change easier.

Things to Do with Boards and Committees

If you have the gift for working with official groups within organizations, then you will probably be on a church board or committee. It may be that you do not have this gift, for not everyone does. If you don't then it might be best for you to follow the suggestion made earlier that you no longer serve in official capacities in the organizational structure of your church. There are many other places you can be about the work of developing a disciple-forming community.

If serving on a board or committee is not your gift, don't feel guilty about it. Simply accept the fact that God intends for you to work in other arenas! If this is a gift of yours, however, use that gift to encourage new perspectives and new behaviors by the board and its members. Here are some suggestions for ways you might do that.

Encourage the board or committee to move away from a business-only approach to its work and become a spiritual community. Charles Olsen calls for a change in the perspective church board members bring to their role: "The individual board member is not to see her- or himself as merely a program manager serving the pastoral CEO or as a political representative of other interests, but as a *spiritual leader* with gifts and power to act."[1] Olsen encourages the development of four new practices for church boards: personal faith story telling, biblical reflection, prayerful discernment for making decisions, and visioning the future for planning. As these are developed, he believes, the nature of the board will change and that change will influence everything: "If the board can move beyond 'business as usual' into the experience of active and energized faith, it will model and lead in ways that impact the whole church. If the board becomes a community of spiritual leaders, the church is bound to feel its effect."[2] Olsen's book, *Transforming Church Boards into Communities of Spiritual Leaders*, is a helpful guide for anyone seeking to enhance the spiritual dimension of church boards.

Look at ways in which the work of the board encourages deepening, equipping, and ministering. Use the chart in appendix B to assess the ways efforts of the board do and can encourage deepening, equipping, and ministering in the life of the congregation. There may be some surprises in store for you when you do this. When I have shared this model in workshops, people have often been amazed at the many ways in which deepening, equipping, and ministering were happening in their churches. Often they realized that many of the significant deepening, equipping, and ministering experiences happened not because of planned programs, but in the more informal aspects of the congregation's life. Others have realized as they did this assessment that it is difficult to divide these three elements among the church boards. Some have even become frustrated at the rigid delineation of responsibilities that keeps the boards in their churches limited to certain restricted areas. Members of a Board of Christian Education, for example, realized that their responsibility for nurturing children as disciples couldn't be fulfilled appropriately without attention to worship, but worship was the deacons' responsibility, not theirs.

Do Bible studies on discipleship. Boards can begin to develop a new understanding of their role in forming disciples as they are exposed to biblical accounts of discipleship. The material in chapter 2 provides biblical background that can be helpful here. Also appendixes C and D can be used by boards to look at qualities of Jesus and the early church. These can be used to initiate a discussion of how these qualities appear in your congregation.

Use the qualities of disciple-forming congregations to shape your work. Use appendix E to get a picture of the state of the qualities of disciple-forming congregations in your church. Once you have shared the results with board members, decide on an area to which you want to devote time and energy. It might be good to work in two areas—one in which you can produce results fairly quickly in order to develop a sense of accomplishment and another in which the challenge is greater.

Let things die. Sooner or later every board struggles with what to do when there are not enough volunteers to maintain a traditional program for which it is responsible. Don't be afraid to let that program die. It may have outlived its effectiveness and never return. Or perhaps the leaders need to rest a year or two before they are ready to undertake the responsibility again. It is not a sign of failure to end a program. In fact, it may be a sign of emerging new life!

Present the vision of disciple-forming. Teaching, preaching, and group studies are all ways in which you can spread the word about the congregation as a disciple-forming community. Determine which of these you think will be most effective in your church and begin to make plans. Presenting the vision isn't just a matter of talking about it, however. In addition to sessions such as these, decide on ways in which you can demonstrate what a disciple-forming congregation is all about. You might begin this with working on gift discovery or by starting small groups that model prayer, action, sharing and learning. It might also be possible for those who share a common concern for community ministry to form a group to do that. No matter what you do, it is important to take an activist stance. Don't get bogged down in seeking approval from an array of people and committees. When you see what needs doing, do it!

THINGS TO DO WITH THE ENTIRE CONGREGATION

Being a disciple-forming community requires the involvement of the entire congregation. It isn't a program a single board and some people can do. It is the congregation's identity—its reason for being. Because this is true, at some point in the process of change the entire congregation will need to become involved. The entire congregation will need to decide this is what it is, what it wants to be. As the process of change has spread from individuals to kindred spirits to boards and committees, more and more people have become involved. Some people will continue to be more involved and more committed to the process than others, but the opportunity for involvement needs to be offered to everyone.

It may take some time to reach the point of involving the entire congregation in this process. The experience of one church I know is not uncommon. It began with the weekly prayer and Bible study with just the pastor and one member. As training events were offered, church members were invited to attend. Over the period of two years, a number of other church members began to develop a desire for change that would bring a deeper spirituality and a greater commitment to mission involvement to the church. Not everyone who attended the training events felt that way, but those who did continued to talk with each other about their hopes. When the denomination offered the opportunity of an intentional process of congregational renewal, there was a small group of people ready to become involved. That in turn led to the development of a new vision for the church and a new way of structuring the church in order to make that vision possible. The small group continued to meet but also began to share their vision with individuals and boards and committees in the church. Not everyone was as enthusiastic as they were. Some were opposed. But the process of sharing made certain everyone had the opportunity to share opinions, affirmations, and concerns.

The following suggestions provide ways of involving the broader congregation. In most cases a leader team, perhaps a board or committee or a group formed specifically for this purpose, will implement them. The suggestions differ from those in the previous section, however, in that their aim is to bring maximum participation.

Develop a picture of your congregation as a disciple-forming community. The entire congregation can also use the assessment tool in appendix E that was suggested earlier for board use. It will provide a wealth of information on how members of your congregation are being formed as disciples. Use the information you receive to build on your strengths and improve upon your weaknesses.

Make a commitment to enhance selected congregational qualities. The list of qualities of a disciple-forming congregation can also be used to engage the entire congregation in a process of decision making. Not everyone will agree on all the qualities. You can, however, begin to work on those that have the broadest support. As you work in one area it will become easier to move into others areas at a later time.

Undertake a major assessment and planning process. Some people like to inch their way into change. Others like to plunge. At some point in the process, however, it will likely be helpful for the congregation to undertake a comprehensive assessment and planning process. The material in this book can get you started with that, but other resources will be needed as well.[3]

All of these will require a significant amount of work, but when you have finished the process you will have a helpful and detailed picture of your congregation that will enable you to make important decisions about moving into the future as a disciple-forming community.

❖

As the title of this chapter implies, these entry points are places to begin. The decisions about which suggestions to use, how to use them, and what to do next rest with you. Like any good guidebook, we can provide some helpful information, but you will have to make the decisions yourself. It's an exciting journey, this process of becoming a disciple-forming community. It's full of challenges—some of which can't be anticipated or described in any book, no matter how good and comprehensive. Don't panic, though. You've got more than a guidebook with you on this journey. You've got The Guide. It's that presence that makes the journey possible. It's that presence that turns the journey into a pilgrimage!

Nine ❖ Perspectives on a "Post-" World

W<small>E'VE COME A LONG WAY. WITH ALL WE'VE LEARNED</small> along the way it might be helpful for us to look a bit more deeply at some of the factors that led us to begin this journey in the first place. In chapter 1 we looked very briefly at some of the key features of this world, which we described as both post-Christendom and postmodern. In this chapter we'll look in more detail at the end of Christendom and the demise of modernity in order to gain a deeper understanding of the forces that are at work that demand the reshaping of our understanding of what it means to be a church. In keeping with our guidebook motif, this is a chapter for those who want to explore one aspect of our journey more fully. If this isn't of great interest to you, you may want to move on to the next chapter, which looks at a biblical time very similar to our own.

SIGNS OF THE NEW LAND

The signs of being in a different world are all around us. Some point to these signs in distress, others in hope. For some they are signs of moral decay and omens of a decadent future. For others they are signs of new possibility. In some cases, the signs seem to be incompatible, if not mutually contradictory. Rather than joining the debate over the signs and their value, however, let's begin by simply looking at some of them.

There is a secular mindset. Whether it is decried as "secular humanism" or applauded as a movement away from a culture dominated by religious mythology, the world we live in is an increasingly secular one. It is dominated by the assumption that our essential needs can all be met through the secular pursuits of science, politics, and economics, which are governed by scientific principles. These are the arenas in which the important things are accomplished. These disciplines provide the perspective from which people view their lives and determine meaning and purpose. From a Christian perspective this secular mindset leads to idolatry. Materialism, consumerism, and militarism are the gods of the secular age. This is where people look in order to secure the happiness and security they seek. The new car, the shopping mall, American flags, and yellow ribbons are the symbols on the altar at which secular society worships. They have a pervasive and profound impact, shaping the lives even of those who are actively involved in the church.

There is a newly emerging understanding of truth. Despite what seems to be an abiding faith in the ability of technology to solve all our problems, there is a growing disenchantment with the modern notion of truth. In the secular, scientific world truth was seen as something that could be determined through logical reasoning. More and more truth is being seen as something more than intellectual knowledge. It is not just rationally determined but encompasses our subjective experience. Rational thinking is still important, but it no longer has the final say. What we feel "in the gut" is part of the picture of truth by which we live.

Because subjective experience is important, the context in which we live takes on new meaning. That context is a relational one. It comes from the interaction of people in community. It is communal more than individual. It shapes our perspective, understanding, purpose, and meaning. It is our context that provides the subjective experience that shapes each person's understanding of the truth. This means that talk about universal truth is increasingly seen as impossible, if not laughable.

I grew up in a Baptist church in Rhode Island and have served Baptist churches in Massachusetts, Ohio, New York, and New Jersey. Along the way I have spent significant time in Baptist churches all around the United States. There is much they have in common, but in many ways they are different. In many ways their understanding of the truth about what it means to be a church is very different. It is each church's individual context that shapes those differences. Its individual history, its cultural setting, and its social perspective have a far greater role in shaping the kind of church it is than any other factor. There may well be absolute truth, but no one of these churches (or any church) has absolute knowledge of that truth, because its grasp of the truth is determined by its context.

There is a greater acceptance of diversity. The great variety of contexts that shape our understandings of truth demands, at the very least, an acceptance of diversity. In the emerging world, however, positive appreciation of diversity is more likely. It is this diversity that exposes us to differing perspectives and leads us to a more profound understanding of meaning. Great diversity leads almost inevitably to what seems to be chaos. On the surface there appears to be no overarching truth or purpose, nothing to bring diverse claims and experiences together under one theme. There is no logical way to "get a handle on things," to organize or systematize them. In the old world this chaos needed to be avoided at all cost. In the emerging world, however, there is a growing realization that even in this seeming chaos there is an ordering principle that can emerge over time and that, in fact, this seeming chaos is essential to growth and renewal.[1]

There is a growing suspicion of institutions, authorities, and hierarchies. The hierarchical institutions created in the old world are suspect in the new. The principle reason for this is that they establish power relationships based on the assumption that those at the top of the hierarchy have access to the truth and need to use their power to coerce others into accepting that truth. If the very idea of absolute truth is questioned, structures that are geared to imposing one person's truth upon someone else are suspect. Structures in the emerging world are networks in which power relationships are severely limited, open communication is enhanced, and varieties of context and perspective are honored.

There is a growing concern for the spiritual. Part of the subjective experience that the emerging world honors is the spiritual. This is not exclusively Christian spirituality. It takes in a wide variety of beliefs and encompasses a great variety of experiences. In all its forms, however, spirituality is affirmed as a valid dimension of life. Genuine spirituality opens the door to mystery. Not everything can be understood. Sometimes we simply stand in awe of the unknowable. This is in opposition to the old view that believed the unexplained always had an explanation that had not yet been discovered—that it was nothing more than another object for observation that would lead to a logical and comprehensive analysis and understanding.

There is a strong desire for experience and participation. If the mind is not the source of truth and the arbiter of reality, if objective observation is not possible, then life in the laboratory has limited meaning. If context is important, involvement in that context is needed. If detached analysis doesn't lead to truth, then participation is essential. All of this leads to the desire to become involved in the actual doing of things. Whether it's sports or mission trips, there is in the emerging world a great desire for participation.

There is an appreciation of the humorous and ironic. In this world of diversity and uncertainty humility is essential. That humility is expressed and enhanced in the humorous and ironic, which are affirmations of the inconsistencies, the limitations, and, at times, even the absurdities of life.

There is only marginal interest in Christianity. There is a great wondering about faith. While a concern for spirituality grows, there is suspicion of the institutional church, as well as a befuddlement by many who haven't found the spiritual vitality they seek within the church. In vast numbers people are simply looking elsewhere to have their spiritual needs met. Much of the reason for this lies in the church's persistent efforts to be taken seriously in the modern world. It has presented faith as logical and rational. It has adapted its teachings to new scientific truths. It has used corporate and psychological models to shape the role of clergy. It has served as a prop to the secular state. And yet it still finds itself on the margins of society. Neither the institution nor its clergy are looked to for leadership in the vital issues of the day. Even in the few places where this happens, it does so much less frequently than in the past.

❖❖

The reasons behind all these realities lie in the profound changes that are taking place in American life and culture. These changes began in the mid-twentieth century, accelerated as the century neared its end, and continue at an ever increasing pace today. While profoundly diverse, they can most easily be described as the end of Christendom and the demise of modernity. We have entered a post-Christendom, postmodern world. Practices, programs, and organizational models that served well in the old world do so no longer. The post-Christendom, postmodern world in which we live necessitates profound changes in both the understanding and the practice of faith in the congregation.

As a pastor I encountered this reality almost every day. It was apparent in the personal dislocation so many in the congregation felt—a sense that somehow things were different and it was hard to feel that your feet were securely planted any more. It was a primary cause of many of the tensions that members of the congregation experienced with each other and with me as their pastor—because the old rules about the roles we were to play no longer made sense and couldn't be implemented, but no one knew what the new rules were. It led to ever-increasing frustration for all of us as we continually tried to do the things that had always worked before and they had no impact at all—and in many cases actually made things worse. It was difficult in these circumstances not to resort to playing the blame game and, in all honesty, there were times we did. What others in the congregation and I gradually came to understand, however, is that it wasn't really anyone's fault at all. Rather, we were dealing with a situation in which it wasn't just that the rules had been changed, but the game itself was entirely different. We were attempting to play the modern Christendom church game, but the real game was about the post-Christendom, postmodern church.

Post-Christendom, postmodern—those terms themselves say much about the state in which we find ourselves. The only way to describe it is to say what it is not. It is *not* a modern world any more; neither is it the world of Christendom. It's not a world that believes the scientific method can objectively determine universal truth or that progress is inevitable. Neither is it a world in which Christian perspectives and values shape the culture in which we live. It is a "post-" world.

THE END OF CHRISTENDOM

It all started on a fourth century battlefield. That's where Constantine saw a vision of a cross and led his troops into battle in the belief that the God of this cross would lead him to victory over his foes. The triumph that followed ushered in the Age of Christendom. In gratitude to the God he believed responsible for his victory he decreed that Christianity would be the state religion. After 300 years of being outside the realms of power and suspect by those in authority, Christians entered a new world of prestige and influence.

The relationship between church, state, and culture took many forms during the Age of Christendom. In the Western world, however, a common thread throughout the Age was a close identification of the perspective, values, and interests of the church with those of society. Sometimes the relationship was so complete that the state persecuted those who did not adhere to the particular tenets of the particular form of Christianity it was advocating at a particular time. At other times the relationship was more subtle, but still profound. This is probably most clearly seen in the "Protestant Establishment" in the United States. Even without an established state church, Protestant thinking, values, and mores were so broadly accepted that the state took on the role of encouraging and enforcing them. Thus, there were blue laws to keep Sunday a day of rest and the recitation of the Lord's Prayer in public schools to instill the right values in children. Historian Robert Handy summarizes the vision that propelled the Protestant alliance with culture through most of American history:

> From the beginning American Protestants entertained a lively hope that some day the civilization of the country would be fully Chris-

tian. The ways in which the hope was expressed and the activities it engendered varied somewhat from generation to generation, but for more than three centuries Protestants drew direction and inspiration from the vision of a Christian America.[2]

In the Age of Christendom—when it was possible to assume a general participation in churches, a general acceptance of faith, a general identification with Christian values—mission could be assumed to be something we did "out there" and "for them." It was away from where we were, with people who were different from us. It was for those who did not have the advantage that we had of living in a "Christian" society and culture, who had not yet had the opportunity to hear the good news of the saving grace of Jesus Christ. In such a world the thing to do was to send missionaries. Denominational structures were developed to support that work. Stewardship was promoted in order to provide the funding needed for the sending. The sign of true faithfulness in a church was the size of its "mission budget," for that proved they were selfless and more concerned about others than themselves.

Loren Mead has identified what he calls the Christendom Paradigm[3] that governed the understanding of the church during the Age of Christendom. Its major beliefs were:

1. There was no distinction between secular and sacred.
2. Mission happened far off, conducted by those employed by church and/or state to bring others into the political/religious realm.
3. The congregation was a parish to which everyone within a specified geographic area belonged.[4]
4. The need for expansion and control produced an unrelenting drive for unity of belief and between church and state.
5. The life of the entire community was intended to nurture the religion of its members.
6. The calling of the laity was to be good citizens.

All of this began to break down as early as the Reformation, which destroyed the notion of one true Christian religion accepted by everyone. The major characteristics of the Christendom Paradigm, however, continued within each of the newly created fragments of the former Empire. The one religion was gone, but in this new setting each state sought to create the church-state-culture alliance of the Christendom Paradigm within its borders. That paradigm is becoming increasingly unworkable in a world in which even within individual nations there is significant diversity. In the United States, for example, we can no longer assume that everyone (or even a majority) is Christian and that the community in which we live is built upon and supports basic Christian values. But still, the paradigm has immense power to shape our perception of reality and the way in which the church should function.

> The paradigm's importance for us lies in the fact that most of the generation that now leads our churches grew up with it as a way of thinking about church and society. And all the structures and institutions that make up the churches and the infrastructure of religious life, from missionary societies to seminaries, from congregational life to denominational books of order and canons, are built on the presupposition of the Christendom Paradigm— not the ancient, classical version of the paradigm as it was understood centuries ago, but the version that flourished with new life in the nineteenth and early twentieth centuries.[5]

Over the years, changing circumstances led to adjustments in the Christendom Paradigm, helping to create this new version of the paradigm to which Mead refers. One group, more often those considered "liberal," has approached the world from a largely secular perspective while still using the language of faith. Social activism was conducted as a community organizer would do it and therapy was done using the tools of contemporary psychology. There was an overlay of religious language, but in both cases it was the secular schools of thought, rather than faith, that shaped involvement. At the other end of the spectrum, more the province of conservatives, there has in recent years been the attempt to reinvigorate the alliance of faith and culture. This approach is explicitly religious and seeks to reestablish what it sees as the traditional Christian foundation for American public life. It is seen in organizations such as the Christian Coalition and in specific issue movements, such as those advocating a constitutional amendment to permit state-supported prayer in public schools.

While seemingly in opposition to each other, both these approaches operate from within a Christendom Paradigm that seeks an alliance of religion and culture. One does it by adopting the current secular cultural mindset, the other by seeking to re-establish Christian values and perspectives as the basis for society. Both, however, assume the alliance.

The changes that have taken place in the world as the age of Christendom comes to an end force us to give up ways of thinking about the church that have been in place for more than 1500 years. Loren Mead sets the challenge before us:

> We are surrounded by the relics of the Christendom Paradigm, a paradigm that has largely ceased to work. But the relics hold us hostage to the past and make it difficult to create a new paradigm that can be as compelling for the next age as the Christendom Paradigm has been for the past age.[6]

Change will not be easy.

The Demise of Modernity

Closely related to the decline of Christendom, but still distinct, is the emergence of postmodernity.[7] Before we can understand what postmodernity is all about, however, we need to look briefly at the modern world. This, even though we are all intimately familiar with it, is not an easy thing to do. Part of the reason for that is that a good deal of the discussion about modernity and postmodernity has taken place in the realm of philosophy and is therefore relatively inaccessible (and uninteresting) to most of us. A more important reason, however, is that because modernity has been the context of our lives for so long it is difficult to grasp any other way of thinking about things. Modernity has provided the perspective from which we view everything and we have taken it for granted. We think of the insights of modernity as common sense or as simply the way things are and have to be. The postmodern challenge encourages us to stop doing that and to begin to think differently about how the world and we are put together.

The driving force of modernity was the idea of progress. This idea was a new way of thinking about life that first arose at the time of the Renaissance and came to prominence with the Enlightenment, beginning in the seventeenth century. Since then it has become a basic assumption about the way things work in the world. Deeply instilled in all moderns, ourselves included most likely, is the belief that humankind will continue to advance, life will continue to get better, our standard of living will continue to rise.

Behind this thinking lies a deep faith in science and the scientific method—that is, the objective analysis of the universe, including human beings and the world in which we live. That analysis usually proceeds by pulling things apart and looking at them as separate systems. So, for example, in biology human beings came to be seen as a collection of systems (digestive, circulatory, and the rest). In psychology, we were understood to have an id and an ego, a rational side and an emotional side, a physical being and a spiritual being. Some of these are not unique to the modern world, but the combination of them and the extent to which they are taken is. It was also assumed that the world itself was made up of a collection of separate parts, fit together to work as a whole. In other words, in the modern view the whole was nothing more than the sum of its parts. There was a place for everything and everything should be in its proper place. These parts could be analyzed, the truth about them could be discovered, and when they and the truths about them were put together we would know the truth about the whole. That is how the natural order of the universe would be discovered, how the laws of nature would become known.

This scientific analysis by itself, however, was not enough to insure progress. Faith in science had to be joined by faith in technology—the application of scientific knowledge to practical issues. It was technology that fueled progress and an ever-rising standard of living. It was technology that would solve all the problems of living. It would make humans healthier and able to live longer; it would make our lives easier and more comfortable; it would lead us into new worlds of discovery. Technology could even be relied upon to solve the problems that the application of technology had created in the first place, such as disposing of atomic waste or the destruction of the ozone layer.

In order for all of this to work, a number of assumptions about human beings needed to be made. First and foremost is that we are rational beings, as was expressed in René Descartes' dictum, "I think, therefore I am." This is what separates us from animals. It is this rationality that allows us to be detached and dispassionate observers, analyzing systems and discovering the truth about them. In this view, pure logic and unemotional objectivity are what matter most. The rational intellect is what ultimately determines truth.

Another aspect of the modern view of humans is autonomy. This is the belief that we can and should stand on our own. We are masters of the universe, as well as our own fate. The human challenge is to overcome everything that holds us back and to surmount every obstacle placed in front of us in order to be all that we can be.

All things would be possible if this autonomous, dispassionate, knowledgeable human being were able to objectively pursue scientific truth about the universe, the world, and humankind. The truth gathered in this process would usher in a new age of scientific discovery and technological advances that would make the world a better place, as well as sociological and psychological insights that would make people better people.

One other aspect of modernity is important for us to understand. Because the modern mind believed in objectively discoverable truth, this led to a belief in universal truth. The truth discovered through objective, dispassionate, scientific processes applied to everything. It described the way the world was everywhere and for everyone. Because it was Westerners who were discoverers of this truth, they assumed a special role in sharing it with others. Western scientific knowledge, Western values, Western political systems— all constructed through the application of universal truth to concrete issues—needed to be brought to the rest of the world.

The church we know is a product of the modern world. Modernity has shaped it in many ways. Systematic theology can be seen as the church's attempt to fit our beliefs together into one coherent, logical system made up of discrete parts. The hierarchical structures of most churches (even those that claim to be congregational) are attempts to bring order to the system or to control the understanding of truth that has been determined by those who know more. Our attempts to relate Christian faith to the challenges of the world in apologetics are well reasoned, using the framework of modern logical thought to make their case. Our spirituality, particularly in its Protestant versions, is most often rational, lacking a sense of the mystical. Our evangelism, in its more extreme form, is based in spiritual laws, but in almost all forms is based in a modern view of giving specific, concrete answers to questions. Our education is cognitive and based in a classroom model that seeks to impart intellectual knowledge to those who are ignorant, truth to those who need it but don't yet have it. Our mission seeks to bring the faith, thinking, and amenities of the modern world to others. Although none of these has ever been universal in scope, each has done much to shape the dominant religious life of the past century and continues to have significant influence today.

The changes that have taken place in the world as modernity comes to an end force us to give up ways of thinking about faith and the church that have been in place for more than 300 years. Leonard Sweet puts the challenge before us as succinctly as anyone:

> In the midst of one of the greatest transitions in history—from the modern to postmodern—Christian churches are owned lock, stock, and barrel by modernity. They have clung to modern modes of thought and action, their way of embodying and enacting Christian tradition frozen in patterns of high modernity.[8]

Change will not be easy.

SO WHERE DOES THAT LEAVE US?

The end of Christendom and the demise of modernity became increasingly evident during the second part of the twentieth century. The signs of this reality had been present much earlier and at least some had begun to discuss them, but it wasn't until about 50 years ago that the discussion broadened into one that included a number of church leaders, and the issues being discussed began to be felt in the day-to-day life of congregations.

The reality of the end of Christendom became apparent as traditional mainline church membership began to decline and as steps were taken to lessen the influence of Christian practice in American culture. The school prayer decisions of the Supreme Court in 1962–1963, for example, were an acknowledgement that Christian, largely Protestant, practices would no longer receive state sanction.[9]

As the Christendom Paradigm became increasingly shaky, new understandings of mission began to develop. Mission could no longer be viewed as something that happened half a world away, but rather as something right outside our door. Those with whom we need to share the gospel so that they can be touched and transformed by God's love are our neighbors and colleagues at work. They are people who, in outward appearance at least, are very much like us. Many of them are on a quest—they know they have deeply spiritual needs that are not being met.[10] There is, however, nothing at work in the broader culture that will lead them naturally to the church in order to meet this need, because in the post-Christendom world culture no longer supports the values and practices of Christianity. Many of them simply have no idea at all about the most basic beliefs we cherish, no sense at all of the difference the experience of God's love and grace can make in their lives.

This change in our understanding of where mission happens has profound implications for every congregation. It means, for example, that there is no longer any easy delineation between a church's operating budget and its mission budget. If we are doing mission in the community to people who do not know the gospel, then our worship service is mission, our classes and small groups are mission, the way we use our building is mission. Given the reality that much of the money that is given through traditional denominational mission channels is used to fund staff salaries and pay utility bills at denominational offices, it is increasingly difficult to maintain that this form of mission giving is somehow more legitimate than paying for staff and utility bills to support the local mission of the congregation. To take it a step further, if mission is at our doorstep, then we are all missionaries. We all need training to do the work of missionaries. And so we need leaders who can equip and coach us for mission, not just care for us or do mission on our behalf. In the post-Christendom world, laity need to be something more than good citizens and clergy something more than chaplains. It is the ministry of both clergy and laity to be involved in mission.[11]

Similarly, the assumptions of the modern world began to break down early in the twentieth century, and by mid-century a strong critique of modernism began to emerge. Initially limited to philosophical circles, by the end of the century this critique was a widespread cultural reality, impacting perspectives on everything from education to media to politics. We took a look at many of those in the earlier section of this chapter, "Signs of the New Land."

Perhaps most significant of all, however, the understanding of humanity that was the foundation of modernism came under direct challenge. The view of a dispassionate, objective knower seeking after universal truth and using knowledge acquired in the search for the increasing betterment of humankind simply did not stack up against reality. People looked around and were forced to conclude that this simply wasn't true. When left to their own devices, humans seemed inevitably to do more harm than good, bring more violence than peace. The attempt to share the virtues and values of Western democratic truth with others seemed to lead to one war after another. Philosophers also challenged this assumption about human identity by declaring that it was not an innate truth at all, but simply a way of looking at human beings that Western thought had chosen to adopt.

This challenge to human self-understanding had a profound impact—increasing uncertainty and doubt, enhancing fears about ability and worth, amplifying apathy, and contributing to an increased sense of fatalism. Faced with this rather devastating reality, by the end of the century a significant portion of the population opted for cocooning and becoming couch potatoes.

But, it isn't all gloom and doom. In these challenges to modernism a number of positive affirmations and possibilities begin to emerge.

- If there is no one valid worldview, diversity is recognized.
- If the world cannot be scientifically dissected and rationally analyzed in order to discover its truth, there is the potential

for a more holistic understanding of life. Concern for the interrelatedness of all elements of creation enhances our appreciation of others, our understanding of the importance of the environment, and our sense of ourselves as whole beings, not just a collection of parts.

- If context is all-important, then communities of belonging take on a renewed importance, helping to challenge the extreme individualism of modernity.

- If truth is understood as something more than factual information cognitively determined, there is a greater appreciation of the mysterious and spiritual, so faith plays a more important role in human understanding.

- If authority is based in trust and authenticity rather than position and power, it increases the possibilities that those with authority will seek to serve others.

- If the old ways no longer serve their purpose, we are forced into a stance of openness that can attune us more fully to seeking God's presence and work in our midst.

❖

The experiences of people of faith who have faced similar times of dislocation—similar opportunities to rediscover God's call to them—are among the great resources we have available to us as we attempt to meet this challenge. It is to one such an experience that we turn our attention in the next chapter.

Ten ❖ A View from Exile

WE LIVE IN LIMBO. THIS NEW POST-CHRISTENDOM, postmodern world is unfamiliar and strange to us. Even when we are able to affirm the renewed importance of some of the basic elements of our faith, even though we reclaim the church's core purpose of forming disciples, there is still much that makes us feel like aliens living in a foreign land. It is impossible to underestimate the impact this has on us, our way of life, and our faith. Those things that once provided the cultural meaning, identity, and security that we depend upon are no longer there for us. We can try to cling more firmly to the old world and ways that are slipping away, but that strategy has no long-term viability. We will only be able to hang on so long and then everything will slip from our grasp. A better, although not easy, approach is to accept the reality we face— to admit that a new world is emerging and we need to find a way to live in it. We may always exist as strangers or aliens, but we do need to find a way to live in it.

DEALING WITH DISLOCATION

In such a time, with such a challenge before us, we need help from those who have been there before us—people who have experienced the same kind of dislocation, people who tried to find new ways of being and believing in the midst of that dislocation. We won't be able to copy them. Their specific answers probably won't work for us. But we can learn from them as we listen to their questions and watch them as they search for answers. We can also take heart from them, knowing that others have been through what we are going through and have found their way.

The people of the exile were a dislocated people. They, too, knew what it meant to have traditional sources of meaning, identity, and security taken away from them. They, too, knew what it meant to need to find a new way to worship, a new expression of their faith. They are, after all, the ones who first asked, "How could we sing the Lord's song in a foreign land?" (Psalm 137:4). Knowing a bit more about their experience will help us deal more effectively with our own.

❖

It was by most accounts the worst of times. The nation had been conquered and the king deposed. The temple had been destroyed, the priesthood decimated. Any pretext of independent nationhood was gone. Any vestige of being God's chosen and therefore unconquerable people was vanquished. Those things that had held the nation together, giving it security, purpose, and self-understanding were no longer viable. It was the worst of times.

It is still not completely clear what really happened in Israel in the sixth century before Jesus was born. The details are hard to come by because the biblical accounts are not complete and archeological evidence is limited. What is known is that when the Babylonians conquered Jerusalem in 597 BCE the king and others were sent to Babylon.[1] For conduct far less than loyal to the conqueror, the new king and other leaders were also deported and the city was at least partially destroyed in 587. The extent of the destruction is not known, although it appears to have been significant. The actual number of people sent to Babylon is also unclear. The conditions under which those in Babylon and those who remained in Judah lived are impossible to determine precisely. It is clear, however, that this was a time of significant dislocation—politically, economically, and religiously. Those who were deported found themselves in a different country, without their usual means of livelihood and the temple that was central to their religious life. Those who remained lived in a nation that had lost its leaders, its independence, its temple, and its political and economic infrastructure. Both groups also found themselves having to deal with significant questions of faith, for how could they continue to believe in a God whose chosen people had been defeated. Could this God be trusted? Could the power of this God be believed?

The question we bring to the experience of the exile is: how was Israel able to deal with this reality? If we can answer that, we may be able to gain insight for our own experience. The answers to this question, and there are several, were for Israel answers of faith. Each of them dealt not only with their existential situation, but also with their understanding of God.

One way Israel dealt with the situation was to explore the reasons for it. This was both a question about their conduct and God's power. The predominate response of the Old Testaments prophets was to say that the exile happened because of Israel's sin.[2] For Ezekiel that sin was idolatry that rejected the absolute holiness of God. "Mortal, do you see what they are doing, the great abominations that the house of Israel are committing here, to drive me far from my sanctuary?" (Ezekiel 8:6).[3] It was the holiness of God that made it impossible for God to abide Israel's sin. The judgment that came upon Israel was because of this holiness.

Jeremiah saw the sin of Israel more in terms of not trusting in God to provide and refusing to live within the framework of the divine covenant:

> For my people are foolish,
>   they do not know me;
> they are stupid children,
>   they have no understanding.

They are skilled in doing evil,
>   but do not know how to do good.
>
>   Jeremiah 4:22

Although the precise understanding of the nature of the sin differs from prophet to prophet, the essence of the message is clear: Israel's sin led to the exile. God is all-powerful. God is punishing Israel for her sin.

This reaffirmation of the power of God also became the basis for hope. In Ezekiel there was a promise of deliverance based in the holiness of God. It was a promise to bring them into their own land, to give them a new heart and a new spirit, to put God's spirit within them, to be God's people as Yahweh will be their God. The reason for this action had nothing to do with what the people have done. Neither did it have anything to do with God's compassion and love. It was solely a matter of the holiness of God.

> Therefore say to the house of Israel, Thus says the Lord God: It is not for your sake, O house of Israel, that I am about to act, but for the sake of my holy name, which you have profaned among the nations to which you came. I will sanctify my great name, which has been profaned among the nations, and which you have profaned among them; and the nations shall know that I am the Lord, says the Lord God, when through you I display my holiness before their eyes.
>
>   Ezekiel 36:22–23

Jeremiah also brings a word of deliverance based in a belief in the power of God:

> Thus says the Lord:
> I am going to restore the fortunes of the tents of Jacob,
>   and have compassion on his dwellings;
> the city shall be rebuilt upon its mound,
>   and the citadel set on its rightful site.
> Out of them shall come thanksgiving,
>   and the sound of merrymakers.
> I will make them many, and they shall not be few;

I will make them honored, and they shall not be disdained.
Their children shall be as of old,
>   their congregation shall be established before me;
>   and I will punish all who oppress them.
Their prince shall be one of their own,
>   their ruler shall come from their midst;
I will bring him near, and he shall approach me,
>   for who would otherwise dare to approach me?
says the Lord.
And you shall be my people,
>   and I will be your God.
>   Jeremiah 30:18–22

The affirmation of the power of God to bring deliverance to the people reaches its highpoint in Isaiah—here in words we normally associate with Advent, but which would have been great news to a people seeking to return home to Jerusalem, yet afraid of the difficulty of the journey:

A voice cries out:
"In the wilderness prepare the way of the Lord,
>   make straight in the desert a highway for our God.
Every valley shall be lifted up,
>   and every mountain and hill be made low;
the uneven ground shall become level,
>   and the rough places a plain.
Then the glory of the Lord shall be revealed,
>   and all people shall see it together,
>   for the mouth of the Lord has spoken."
>   Isaiah 40:3–5

But there is more to it than the development of theology of sin and deliverance that explained the tragedy Israel had endured while still upholding the power of God. One of the most important functions of the Old Testament prophets was to be a voice for the people in the expression of their concerns and celebrations. That prophetic role is the second part of the answer to our question: How was Israel able to deal with the profound dislocation and suffering of the exile? What was it that enabled the people to come to terms with the experience in a way that led to hope and positive action? What process led them to the point of being able to celebrate and participate in God's "new thing"?

While the word "process" suggests something much neater than what actually took place, it does offer us a way to get a handle on the experience of those in exile. The prophetic accounts suggest several elements in that process. They are not clearly defined and they didn't happen in any set order, but they do suggest a movement that is important. The elements of that movement are: grief/rage, humility, comfort, hope, and action.[4]

Grief/rage. Israel needed to grieve her loss. An important prophetic task was to lead the people in their grieving, to acknowledge and express the pain. The laments of the prophets express the pain of their suffering, directing it at times at God. But God is not the only object of their wrath. Sometimes it is the conquerors. And sometimes the rage is expressed in a way that seems beyond any decency. The most graphic example of this is Psalm 137, which celebrates the possibility that the children of Babylon will be dashed against the rocks. A less gruesome and still deeply poignant expression of that pain is found in Jeremiah, for whom the grief is an intensely personal experience, both as his grief and the grief of God:

> My anguish, my anguish! I writhe in pain!
> > Oh, the walls of my heart!
> My heart is beating wildly;
> > I cannot keep silent;
> for I hear the sound of the trumpet,
> > the alarm of war.
> Disaster overtakes disaster,
> > the whole land is laid waste.
> > > Jeremiah 4:19–20a

> Is there no balm in Gilead?
> > Is there no physician there?
> Why then has the health of my poor people
> > not been restored?
> O that my head were a spring of water,

and my eyes a fountain of tears,
so I might weep day and night
for the slain of my poor people!
Jeremiah 8:22–9:1

In the expression of this grief it becomes possible to have hope. In fact, it is God's response to this grief that provides the basis for Israel's hope:

Thus says the Lord:
A voice is heard in Ramah,
lamentation and bitter weeping.
Rachel is weeping for her children;
she refuses to be comforted for her children,
because they are no more.
Thus says the Lord:
Keep your voice from weeping,
and your eyes from tears;
for there is a reward for your work,
says the Lord:
they shall come back from the land of the enemy
there is hope for your future
says the Lord:
your children shall come back to their own country.
Jeremiah 31:15–17

Humility. Humility is an essential aspect of the prophetic emphasis on Israel's sin. Clearly it takes humility to admit wrongdoing, especially of the profound nature expressed by the prophets. In fact this is the clear requirement that is placed on the people:

Let us lie down in our shame, and let our dishonor cover us; for we have sinned against the Lord our God, we and our ancestors, from our youth even to this day; and we have not obeyed the voice of the Lord our God.

Jeremiah 3:25

Comfort. When the numbness and denial have ended and the grief and rage have been expressed, when the arrogant righteousness has been set aside for humility, then it is possible for the people to be comforted. The prophet, most notably in the words of Isaiah, also offers that comfort:

> Comfort, O comfort my people
>> says your God.
> Speak tenderly to Jerusalem,
>> and cry to her
> that she has served her term,
>> that her penalty is paid,
> that she has received from the Lord's hand
>> double for all her sins.
>> Isaiah 40:1–2

This comfort is from God; it comes in God's time, because God has decided to offer it. That is the promise of the prophet. After the expressions of grief and rage, after the evidence of a humble heart, comfort will come:

> Then shall the young women rejoice in the dance,
>> and the young men and the old shall be merry.
> I will turn their mourning into joy,
>> I will comfort them, and give them gladness for sorrow.
>> Jeremiah 31:13

Hope. Directly tied to comfort is the hope that the prophet provides. In fact, in many cases hope is the source of the comfort, for it is based in God's promise to make things better, to restore the people and the land. This hope is present even in the darkest moments. It is seen, for example, in Jeremiah's purchase of a field even as Jerusalem lies in ruins (Jeremiah 32:9–15). In Jeremiah it reaches its fullest expression in words that promise a new covenant: "I will put my law within them, and I will write it on their hearts; and I will be their God, and they shall be my people" (Jeremiah 31:33).

In Isaiah hope reaches its most eloquent and profound expression. While Isaiah follows Jeremiah in acknowledging the sin of Israel, this is not his major purpose. He seeks, rather, to give the people hope—a hope that motivates them to action. In that effort he draws on all the resources of language at his command to paint pictures that break through old thought patterns and to connect the people to the ongoing work of God in the world:

> Do not remember the former things,
>   or consider the things of old.
> I am about to do a new thing;
>   now it springs forth, do you not perceive it?
> I will make a way in the wilderness
>   and rivers in the desert.
>   Isaiah 43:18-19

The hope for Isaiah is based in the "new thing" that God is doing in leading Israel home. It is a new thing based in what has gone before, to be sure, but it is still new because it is not some past event that is remembered, but a real event in the lives of the people.

Action. For Isaiah, however, the offering of hope for the people is not an end in itself. It is a means of motivating them to action. His speeches are put together to demonstrate God's power, to announce God's intention, and to motivate the people to action so that God's plans may be fulfilled. Hope is the motivator. There is a very close tie between Yahweh and Israel. Yahweh is the one, true, powerful God. And yet, proof of that depends upon the action of Israel. The prophet may announce the making of a way in the wilderness in order to return to Jerusalem, but the proof of God's power to make the way and execute the return depends upon Israel gathering the strength and courage to make the journey back to Jerusalem. Those in exile, however, have little reason to hope, little reason to believe in either God's power or its ability. Israel is on the verge of despair.

Isaiah promises that the strength of these tired, despairing people will be renewed, if only they will join in God's work (Isaiah 40:28-31). He then goes on to convince his listeners of God's power, inviting them to join the cause. The fervor continues, reaching a climax in Isaiah 51 and 52, as the prophet urges the people on:

> Listen to me, you that pursue righteousness (51:1)
> Listen to me, my people (51:4)

Awake, awake, put on strength (51:9)
Rouse yourself, rouse yourself (51:17)
Awake, awake, put on your strength (52:1)
Depart, depart, go out from there! (52:11)

There is reason to act, for God's power is great and the result of their action is clear:

For you shall go out in joy,
    and be led back in peace;
the mountains and the hills before you
    shall burst into song,
        and all the trees of the field shall clap their hands.
Instead of the thorn shall come up the cypress;
    instead of the brier shall come up the myrtle;
and it shall be to the Lord for a memorial,
    for an everlasting sign that shall not be cut off.
                    Isaiah 55:12–13

INSIGHTS FOR OUR EXPERIENCE

The similarities between our time and the time of the exile are, at least on the surface, quite striking. We, too, live in an age of dislocation. The traditional sources of meaning, security, and faith have been lost. For the church, the end of Christendom has profoundly shaken our identity, role, and self-understanding. More broadly, the end of modernity and the entry into a postmodern world has had an equally disorienting impact.

Given these similarities, the exile as image or metaphor can provide insight for our times. Walter Brueggemann suggests that the value of a metaphor is not that it provides a one-to-one correspondence (for it does not), but rather that it "proceeds by having only an odd, playful, and ill-fitting match to its reality, the purpose of which is to illuminate and evoke dimensions of reality which will otherwise go unnoticed and therefore unexperienced."[5] It is in that spirit that we can best approach our reflection on the exile. We will, in a very real sense, be playing with the ideas, for this is a time for exploring and probing, a time for wondering and bouncing ideas around. It is in this kind of playfulness that new insight, perhaps even new truth, appears.

Perhaps the most profound and most needed insight is the obvious one. There was in the biblical writers a profound sense of God being at work in everything they were experiencing. In the destruction, in offering comfort, in providing new reason for hope, God was at work. The secular mindset of our time sometimes makes it difficult, even for people of faith, to see God present and active in the experiences of the world. But this is the point on which everything else hinges. We cannot draw on the amazing resources and insights of our faith tradition unless we first believe that God is at work in our lives and world, even as God was in biblical times.

When we begin to see that way, we are led to consider and "play with" notions that might not otherwise come to mind because they seem too far-fetched. Are we, for example, willing to consider the possibility of God being at work in destruction—especially in the destruction of the established institutions of religion, such as individual congregational or denominational structures. According to the prophetic view, God was behind the destruction of the temple. There is, of course, the later view that supports the rebuilding of the temple, but it is important not to rush there too quickly, not before we have grasped the full impact of the temple's destruction. To take this perspective seriously is to be open to the reality that our experience of exile today is, at least in part, a result of God's work to dismantle the old institutions of religion. It may be that, like the temple, they have become self-serving rather than God-serving and therefore need to give way to something new, something better able to participate in God's mission in the world. Some have said we live in a postdenominational age. The struggle for survival in countless local congregations is evident. Is God about the systematic dismantling of these old structures? As with all prophetic claims this one cannot be proved and many good arguments can be offered to challenge it. But certainly denominations and local congregations can make no greater claim to God's continued blessing than did the temple. That would suggest, at the very least, that contemporary exiles should be open to the possibility.

It might also be helpful for us to consider what generation of exiles we are. Are we among the first generation, those who experienced directly the loss of the structures and images of meaning, who continue to grieve their loss, who experience a great emptiness because nothing has yet replaced them? Or, might we be among the second generation—people who have heard the stories but didn't experience them directly, people who have grown up in a foreign land and learned to accommodate to it, people who are not all that clear what is alien and what is not, people who have found some measure of comfort even though they know deep down it is not "the way it is supposed to be"? It could well be that we are, in fact, members of both generations. In the broader cultural picture, we are those who are experiencing the breakdown of modern perspectives, who have experienced firsthand that the old ways of thinking and understanding simply don't work anymore.

There is a sense in which this is true for those in the church as well. Most of us have firsthand experience with the decline of Christendom and the difficulty of functioning in a post-Christendom world. And yet, might it be that the primary connection here is not with the post-Christendom world, but with Christendom itself? Might it be that this world of close alliance of church and culture is a "Babylon" in which it is difficult, if not impossible, for the church to be what it is called to be? Might the struggle of the church today be that we have learned to accommodate to an alien culture, that we have lost a clear sense of the way in which it is foreign to the gospel and have grown comfortable in the way of life we established? Could it be that we are the ones who grew up in exile, never knowing what "home" was like, making do with what we had, confused about what was faith and what was the propaganda of Babylon? Now Babylon has fallen, but we'd just as soon stay where we are, rather than seeing this as the opportunity to become part of God's new thing.

It is also intriguing to reflect on the exile as the experience that for all intents and purposes marks the end of Israel as a political entity. The kingship had come to an end. There was no longer the alliance of priest and king that was central to Israel's self-understanding and her political and religious identity. Even following the Restoration, Israel was nothing more than a vassal state, part of one or another nation's empire. Its days as a political entity were over, but its days as a religious community apart from the state were just beginning. What does this have to say to the exile of American Christendom? Our exile, too, may mark the end of the alliance of priest and king that was inherent in Christendom, of God and country that exists in American ideology. There is no longer an assumed position of the church in American life. If the church is to have influence in the post-Christendom world it will be by neither might nor power. Those who grieve this loss can find some solace in the exile experience; those who welcome it can find a new challenge. A renewed sense of life as a religious community rather than a political and cultural presence can lead to new ways of faithfulness and witness.

The issue of power—particularly the power of God—is also a parallel one. One of the great struggles of the exile was coming to terms with what appeared to be God's defeat. The question it presented to Israel was "Is this God powerful enough to rely on?" The question is a real one in churches today. What happens in your church when someone suggests that if a particular project is God's will the resources needed to do it will be provided? Is it God's power we rely on or is it the power of strategic planning processes, fundraising consultants, the latest growth gimmick, our own programming expertise, or a good preacher? It's a question few people are willing to ask and many of those who do are willing to answer with platitudes. But for us, as for the Israelites, it is a question that demands both our attention and an honest answer. Do we believe God has the power?

Ezekiel's insistence on the holiness of God provides yet another takeoff point for consideration. We have become so focused on the caring and supportive God, the socially concerned God, the good-shepherd-who-lightens-our-burdens God, that we often lose sight of the holy God who will not be mocked, who destroys and restores for no other purpose than the reputation of God's holy name. In the final analysis God is mocked any time we worship something less than all God is. When God is used to justify a nice building and an inwardly focused chaplaincy ministry, consumerist values and nationalistic arrogance, God is mocked, God's holiness is defiled. The notion that God is no longer present in the temple because of its profane worship might go a long way in explaining the lack of spiritual vitality of many of today's churches. But if Ezekiel is to be believed, it does not stop with mere absence. God works in much more dramatic ways to make people aware of the ways in which they have profaned God's name and to preserve divine holiness. It is something to ponder.

Finally, we turn to the insights that come from the movement through grief/rage, humility, comfort, hope, and action that helped Israel deal with the realities of the exile. This movement offers an understanding for our own needs; it provides suggestions for the work of both worship and pastoral care in these days.

Grief/rage. We're not very good at this. Our worship focuses on the positive, except when it comes to the list of prayer concerns. Our words are consistently upbeat. We may grieve a personal loss, but there is little genuine corporate sense of grief over those things that have been lost to all of us—those days and ways that have passed and will never come again. There is even less of a willingness to express rage. Somehow it doesn't seem very "Christian." And it certainly is dangerous. It would do us well to recover the prophetic sense of grief and rage—even to lash out unreasonably if that is what it takes to break out of the numbness. It would do us well to preach more from Lamentations, more from the psalms of lament. The preacher in our midst could lead us in our grieving, could help us express our rage at all we have lost.

Humility. Certainly our experience of exile in these days results from something far more than our own sin. But that does not discount the need for humility and confession. As people, as a church, we have been something less than what God called us to be. In that "something less" we have contributed to the suffering that is a part of our experience. The biblical witness calls us to face that reality, to confess, and to change. We need to do it for those we have injured. We need to do it for ourselves. For without this humility we cannot be open to the gifts God is ready to bestow.

Comfort. The first of these gifts is comfort. The expressions of grief and humility need to come first. This isn't cheap comfort that enables us to feel good all the time. There is a notion afoot in modern Christianity that maintains that to be attuned to God and God's will is to know peace and joy, to always be comforted. The exile experience should disabuse us of that notion. This comfort is real nonetheless. It is the comfort of the community in which grief and humility are real. It is the comfort of the community that believes in both the power and holiness of God. The comfort comes in a word, a gesture. But it comes only if the word is spoken and the gesture is made at the right time. It comes only after the grief and humility, only when the community is real.

Hope. When comfort is real, hope is possible. This hope is from God. It is not about our wishes or about the way we want things to be. It is about God's vision. In fact, the hope of Isaiah came as a disconcerting word to many in Babylon. It was not the kind of hope they wanted because it was a challenging hope, a disruptive hope. It is a hope that can only be heard when we are ready to seek, ready to listen. That is why comfort is essential for us as well. But the word does come, and it is invariably a word about newness. Of course, it will draw on what has been—the traditions and practices of the past—but God will give it a twist that makes it live again in ways we didn't think possible. And that is real hope.

Action. That kind of hope motivates. It leads us into action. Often it doesn't come easy. Isaiah needed to work hard at it, and so will we. It is this action that ultimately redeems the struggle and the suffering of exile. Without that experience we would not understand fully enough, we would not feel deeply enough, to act according to God's hope. Our action is what makes God's new thing possible. Our action is, as Isaiah made clear, what proves the power of God. And it is our action that brings us home again—to our true home in God's kingdom.

❖

This look at the experience of the exile has provided us with insights in the ways another people facing significant dislocation in their lives began to deal with the new realities they faced. We've seen how the resources of their faith both challenged them and provided comfort. In looking at the challenges they faced we have begun to see that we are not alone as we face new challenges related to our understanding of God, our understanding of what it means to faithful, and our willingness to look at "a new thing" God may be asking us to do. We are surrounded by a great cloud of witnesses. In them we see models of faithfulness. Through them we can gather the insight and courage needed as we seek to discover and live out the new thing God is doing in our time and place. We are pilgrims together on a journey that leads us more fully and more deeply into the wonder of God's presence, love, and mission.

❖ Appendix A
Discipleship Assessment
Tool for Individuals

REFLECT BACK ON THE LAST SEVERAL WEEKS AND answer each of these questions. After you have completed them, note the areas of significant involvement as well as those in which you have done little recently. Then, make plans to enhance the weaker areas of your own growth as a disciple.

How has deepening been a part of my life these past weeks?

- In what ways have I grown in my relationship with Christ?
- In what ways have I become more aware of myself as a person—my strengths, my weaknesses, my struggles, my fears, my hopes, the temptations I face, the risks I avoid, the challenges I undertake?
- In what ways have I developed a stronger community in which to share my own faith journey and encourage the journeys of others?
- What can I do to enhance my own deepening?

How has equipping been a part of my life these past weeks?

- Have I discovered new gifts or used old ones in new ways?
- How is my call being lived out? Is it still vital? Am I sensing a new call?
- What have I learned that is important to my living as a disciple?
- What skills have I acquired or improved that increase my ability to live as a disciple?
- What can I do to enhance my own equipping?

How has ministering been a part of my life these past weeks?

- In what ways is the leadership role I play my ministry?
- In what other ways am I living out my discipleship—at home, in the church, at work, and in the community?
- How has my involvement in ministering strengthened my life as a disciple?
- What can I do to enhance my own ministering?

❖ Appendix B
Discipleship Assessment
Tool for Congregations

Deepening—Growing in Relationship	Ways we do this	Things we might do
Experiences that encourage people to grow in their relationship with Jesus Christ through personal and corporate spiritual disciplines. Experiences that might be included here are: • worship • prayer groups • spiritual-growth groups • seasonal-reflection groups (Lent, Advent) • spiritual-emphasis events • seasonal devotional booklets • mentoring relationships • Bible-based sharing groups • spiritual-growth retreats		

Equipping—Growing in Giftedness	Ways we do this	Things we might do
Experiences that encourage people to claim and develop their gifts, discern God's call to them, and acquire the knowledge and skill needed to live out that call faithfully and effectively. Experiences that might be included here are: ♦ Bible-study classes ♦ gift assessment tools and groups ♦ opportunities to experiment using gifts ♦ training opportunitiesto develop skills and gain knowledge ♦ study groups on issues of faith and/or theology		

Ministering—Growing in Service	Ways we do this	Things we might do
Experiences that provide opportunities for people to live out their call and through that both deepen their relationship with Christ and become more effectively equipped to live as Christ's disciples. Experiences that might be included here are: ♦ mission trips ♦ service projects ♦ serving in a leadership role within the church ♦ local mission outreach ♦ volunteer work ♦ understanding work, parenting, and other involvements from a perspective of ministry		

❖ Appendix C
To Be a Disciple of Jesus . . .

IN THE SPACE PROVIDED FOLLOWING EACH STATEMENT offer a prayer reflection about the depth of this dimension of your own relationship with Christ.

To be a disciple of Jesus is to be on a journey.

To be a disciple of Jesus is to serve others.

To be a disciple of Jesus is to be obedient to God in all things.

To be a disciple of Jesus is to make God's work the highest priority in our lives.

To be a disciple of Jesus is to pray.

To be a disciple of Jesus is to live with the conviction that love of God and love of people are intimately tied together.

To be a disciple of Jesus is to show concern for the outcasts of society.

To be a disciple of Jesus is sometimes to suffer.

To be a disciple of Jesus is to live by different rules.

To be a disciple of Jesus is to have faith.

To be a disciple of Jesus is to continue his work of ministry.

❖ Appendix D
The Church Is to Be . . .

In THE SPACE PROVIDED, WRITE YOUR RESPONSE TO EACH of the questions that follow. Then discuss your answers with others in the congregation. What does this suggest to you about areas of growth and change that will aid the congregation in becoming a disciple-forming community?

The church is to be a community that encourages actively seeking God's new thing so that the old can be set aside.

Are we willing to set aside old notions of how Jesus is at work and focus on discovering what it means to be his witnesses now?

The church, empowered by the Spirit, is to be a community of passion committed to sharing about Jesus.

Would anyone ever think members of our congregation were drunk because of their passion for Jesus?

The church is to be a community of deep devotion, not only to Jesus, but also to each other—a devotion demonstrated in a depth of sharing.

Is our congregation one in which there is an intimacy of sharing?

The church is to be a community that understands that what it offers to the world is unique because of the power of Jesus at work in and through its members.

Are we clear about what we cannot offer others even though they ask for it and what, in the name of Jesus Christ, we do have to offer?

The church is to be a community that trusts in the power of the Holy Spirit to enable it to live boldly in order to participate in God's mission in the world.

In the face of opposition and imprisonment for our faith, would it be boldness for which we prayed?

The church is to be a community in which mission determines both leadership positions and those who fill them.

Is our effective engagement in mission the main reason for the roles and structures of our congregation?

The church is to be a community that sees things differently because of Jesus and lives according to the way it sees.

Do we have the courage of our teachings?

The church is to be a community that never ceases to attend to its mission.

Do we use the difficulties and trials we face as new opportunities to witness?

The church is to be a community that rejects the world's currency for God's economy of grace.

Have we eliminated any notion of money as the necessary prerequisite for mission and replaced it with one that believes that the power of the Spirit is sufficient?

The church is to be a community that sends its members into places where they will encounter those for whom the gospel can make a difference.

Are we willing to listen to the Spirit and go where the Spirit tells us to go in order to share the gospel, even if it seems ludicrous?

The church is to be a community of diverse opinions and practices based in a common devotion to Jesus and a shared commitment to his mission.

Are we willing to talk together about our different opinions and practices in order to discover new ways of being faithful to our mission?

The church is to be a community that supports its members as they translate the teachings of Jesus into concrete ways of living in the world.

Are we willing to challenge the social and economic practices of the world in order to remain faithful to Jesus?

The church is to be a community that lives and dies in the faith that God's mission will be fulfilled.

Do we have absolute confidence in the power of God's Word to reach, touch, and transform everyone?

❖ Appendix E
Qualities of the Disciple-
Forming Congregation

MARK EACH OF THE STATEMENTS 1–5 ACCORDING TO how accurately it describes your congregation, with 1 meaning "not at all" and 5 meaning "completely."

_____ Spiritual Vitality

There is within our congregation, both personally and corporately, a deep desire to grow in relationship with Christ and to discern and respond to God's call.

_____ Vital, Transforming Worship

The worship services of our church provide for both members and newcomers a powerful experience of the transforming power that comes through an encounter with the holy.

_____ A Focus on God's Mission

The primary concern of our church, expressed both individually and corporately, is for those who are not members.

_____   Gifts and Call as the Basis for Ministry

Our church pays careful attention to the discernment and development of God-given gifts and uses these as the basis for determining the involvement of members in ministry.

_____   Shared Ministry

Our ministry, both within and outside the church, is shared by clergy and laity based, not on predetermined roles, but gifts.

_____   Commitment to Equipping

Our congregation has a strong commitment, both emotional and financial, to support the equipping of both laity and clergy for the ministries to which God has called them.

_____   Lean, Permission-Giving Structures

Our church has a minimal organizational structure that functions to encourage and support the involvement of members in ministry.

_____   Holistic Small Groups

Our congregation offers a variety of small group experiences that provide opportunities of prayer, action, learning, and sharing based on particular interests of participants.

❖ Appendix F
Qualities-Related Resources

SPIRITUALITY VITALITY

Foster, Richard. *Celebration of Discipline: The Path to Spiritual Growth*. New York: Harper and Row, 1978.

Pagitt, Doug. *Reimagining Church: A Week in the Life of an Experimental Church*. Grand Rapids, MI: Zondervan, 2003.

Ware, Corrine. *Discover Your Spiritual Type: A Guide to Individual and Congregational Growth*. Herndon, VA: Alban Institute, 1995.

Westerhoff, John. *Spiritual Life: The Foundation for Preaching and Teaching*. Louisville: Westminster John Knox, 1994.

VITAL, TRANSFORMING WORSHIP

Berglund, Brad. *Reinventing Sunday*. Valley Forge, PA: Judson Press, 2001.

Callahan, Kennon L. *Dynamic Worship*. San Francisco: Jossey-Bass, 1997.

Dawn, Marva J. *Reaching Out without Dumbing Down: A Theology of Worship for This Urgent Time*. Grand Rapids, MI: Eerdmans, 1995.

Slaughter, Michael. *Out on the Edge: A Wake-Up Call for Church Leaders on the Edge of the Media Reformation.* Nashville: Abingdon Press, 1998.

Webber, Robert E. *Blended Worship: Achieving Substance and Relevance in Worship.* Peabody, MA: Hendrickson Publishers, 1996.

A Focus on God's Mission

Ford, Kevin Graham. *Jesus for a New Generation: Putting the Gospel in the Language of Xers.* Downers Grove, IL: InterVarsity Press, 1995.

Nixon, Paul. *Fling Open the Doors: Giving the Church Away to the Community.* Nashville: Abingdon Press, 2002.

Payne, Claude E., and Hamilton Beazley. *Reclaiming the Great Commission: A Practical Model for Transforming Denominations and Congregations.* San Francisco: Jossey-Bass, 2000.

Gifts and Call as a Basis for Ministry

Fortune, Don, and Katie. *Discover Your God-Given Gifts.* Grand Rapids, MI: Baker Book House, 1987.

Schwarz, Christian. *The Three Colors of Ministry: A Trinitarian Approach to Identifying and Developing Gifts.* St. Charles, IL: ChurchSmart Resources, 2001.

A Commitment to Equipping

Stevens, R. Paul, and Phil Collins. *The Equipping Pastor: A Systems Approach to Congregational Leadership.* Herndon, VA: Alban Institute: 1993.

Shared Ministry and Mission

Mead, Loren. *Five Challenges for the Once and Future Church.* Herndon, VA: Alban Institute, 1996.

Sweet. Leonard. *Aquachurch: Essential Leadership Arts for Piloting Your Church in Today's Fluid Culture.* Loveland, CO: Group Publishing, 1999.

LEAN, PERMISSION-GIVING STRUCTURES

Easum, William M. *Sacred Cows Make Gourmet Burgers: Ministry Anytime, Anywhere, by Anyone.* Nashville: Abingdon Press, 1995.

Easum, William M., and Thomas G. Bandy. *Growing Spiritual Redwoods.* Nashville: Abingdon Press, 1997.

HOLISTIC SMALL GROUPS

Arnold, Jeffrey. *The Big Book on Small Groups.* Downers Grove, IL: Intervarsity Press, 1992.

Bandy, Thomas G. *Christian Chaos: Revolutionizing the Congregation.* Nashville: Abingdon Press, 1999.

Frazee, Randy. *The Connecting Church: Beyond Small Groups.* Grand Rapids, MI: Zondervan, 2001.

❖ Notes

CHAPTER TWO, BACK TO THE BASICS

1. A. B. Bruce, *The Training of the Twelve* (Edinburgh: T & T Clark, 1877), 16–17.

2. References to the Pharisees are limited and at times conflicting. There are three primary sources: the New Testament, the writings of the historian Josephus, and the writings of the Talmud. See John Bowker, *Jesus and the Pharisees* (Cambridge: Cambridge University Press, 1973), for a description of the sources and translations of Josephus and Talmudic writings.

3. Kathleen Kern, *We Are the Pharisees* (Scottdale, PA: Herald Press, 1995), 18.

4. Robert W. Wall, "The Acts of the Apostles," *The New Interpreter's Bible*, vol. 10 (Nashville: Abingdon Press, 2002), 73.

5. See Wall, 41–42, for a discussion of a number of these views.

6. Ibid., 271.

7. See Mark 16:14–18 and Luke 24:36–49 (along with Acts 1:6–8).

8. Alfred Marshall. *The RSV Interlinear Greek-English New Testament.* (Grand Rapids, MI: Zondervan, 1978), 136.

9. "[It] is not an imperative at all, but rather an aorist passive participle used as a deponent verb. Instead of translating it 'Go,' would it not be better translated 'having gone?'" Harold M. Parker, Jr. "The Great Commission," *Interpretation*, vol. 2, no. 1 (January 1948): 74.

10. See Wall, 503, for a discussion of the use of the word "Gentiles" in this passage and its implications for the mission to Israel.

CHAPTER THREE, THE LIFE OF A DISCIPLE

1. The initial description of these three elements of discipleship is found in my book *Youth Ministry: Making and Shaping Disciples* (Valley Forge, PA: Judson Press, 1986), 45–59. Since that time the concept has evolved considerably. A more recent description of the elements can be found in "2001–2002 Christian Education Planning Guide for American Baptist Churches" (Valley Forge, PA: Educational Ministries, 2001). The description presented here represents a continuing evolution of the concept.

CHAPTER FOUR, THE ELEMENTS OF DISCIPLESHIP

1. Richard Foster, *Celebration of Discipline* (San Francisco: Harper and Row, 1978).

2. A helpful discussion of the spirituality of the desert fathers and mothers can be found in Anselm Gruen, *Heaven Begins Within You: Wisdom from the Desert Fathers* (New York: The Crossroad Publishing Company, 1999).

3. Carlyle Marney, *Priests to Each Other* (Valley Forge, PA: Judson Press, 1974), 74.

4. Parker Palmer, *The Courage to Teach: Exploring the Inner Landscape of the Teacher's Life* (San Francisco: Jossey-Bass, 1998), 97.

5. Ibid., 97.

6. Dietrch Bonhoeffer, *Life Together* (New York: Harper and Row, 1954), 23.

7. Ibid., 112.

8. For a more complete discussion of the importance of holographic programming in the church see C. Jeff Woods, *Congregational Megatrends* (Herndon, VA: Alban Institute, 1996), 121–134, and Margaret Wheatley, *Leadership and the New Science* (San Francisco: Berrett-Koehler, 1999), 112.

CHAPTER FIVE, THE DISCIPLE-FORMING COMMUNITY: PRACTICES

1. This is admittedly a strong statement on the role of community. I make it while still acknowledging all the ways in which communal life can be perverted so that it is destructive and all the ways the reality of the local congregation is far less than what is described here. I make it, however, because the vision of such a community is essential to forming disciples, and recapturing that vision is essential to the future of the church.

2. For a more complete discussion of the twin roles of evangelism and discipleship in the life of the congregation, see my book *Youth Ministry: Making and Shaping Disciples* (Valley Forge, PA: Judson Press, 1986). Although written specifically for youth ministry, the concepts of evangelism and discipleship developed in the book apply more broadly to all age levels in a congregation. In that book I described three elements of evangelism: sharing the gospel, clarifying and interpreting, and encouraging and challenging to accept Christ. I note that many, if not most, of the experiences that are needed for discipleship also provide the experiences of these three elements of evangelism.

3. Morton Kelsey, "Educating Children Spiritually and Psychologically," *Religious Education,* vol. 89, no. 4 (Fall 1994): 530.

4. Ibid., 535.

5. Ronald H. Cram, "Knowing God: Children, Play, and Paradox," *Religious Education,* vol. 91, no. 1 (Winter 1996): 64.

6. Ibid., 70.

7. Stephen D. Jones, *Faith Shaping: Youth and the Experience of Faith* (Valley Forge, PA: Judson Press, 1987), 75.

8. Wenger, Etienne, Richard McDermott and William M. Snyder, *Cultivating Communities of Practice* (Boston: Harvard Business School Press, 2002), 9.

9. Ibid., 27.

10. Ibid., 28.

11. Ibid., 19.

12. Diana Butler Bass, *The Practicing Congregation: Imagining a New Old Church* (Herndon, VA: Alban, 2004), 14.

13. Ibid., 53.

14. Ibid., 99.

15. Craig Dykstra, *Growing in the Life of Faith: Education and Christian Practices* (Louisville: Geneva Press, 1999), 42–43.

16. Dorothy C. Bass, ed., *Practicing Our Faith: A Way of Life for a Searching People* (San Francisco: Jossey-Bass, 1997), 5.

17. Doug Pagitt, *Reimagining Church: A Week in the Life of an Experimental Church* (Grand Rapids, MI: Zondervan, 2003), 26–27.

CHAPTER SIX, THE DISCIPLE-FORMING COMMUNITY: QUALITIES

1. These qualities are drawn from a survey of contemporary literature on congregational renewal and transformation. The books cover a spectrum of theological and methodological approaches. The qualities that were selected represent the common threads that run through all these works: Thomas G. Bandy, *Kicking Habits: Welcome Relief for Addicted Churches, Upgrade Edition* (Nashville: Abingdon Press, 2001); George Barna, *The Habits of Highly Effective Churches: Being Strategic in Your God-Given Ministry* (Ventura, CA: Regal Books, 1999); Rodney Clapp, *A Peculiar People: The Church as Culture in a Post-Christian Society* (Downer's Grove, IL: InterVarsity Press, 1996); William M. Easum, *Dancing with Dinosaurs: Ministry in a Hostile and Hurting World* (Nashville: Abingdon Press, 1993); William M. Easum and Thomas G. Bandy, *Growing Spiritual Redwoods* (Nashville: Abingdon Press, 1997); Stanley Hauerwas and William Willimon, *Resident Aliens: Life in the Christian Colony* (Nashville: Abingdon Press, 1989); Bill Hull, *The Disciple-Making Church* (Grand Rapids, MI: Fleming H. Revell, 1990); Brain D. McLaren, *The Church on the Other Side: Doing Ministry in the Post-Modern Matrix* (Grand Rapids, MI: Zondervan, 2000); Christian A. Schwartz, *Natural Church Development* (Carol Stream, IL: ChurchSmart Resources, 1996); C. Jeff Woods, *Congregational Megatrends* (Herndon, VA: Alban Institute, 1996). Portions of the following appeared in different form in "2002–2003 Christian Education Guide for American Baptist Churches" (Valley Forge, PA: Educational Ministries, 2002).

2. I have not explicitly defined "spirituality" to this point, wishing to allow readers to bring their own understanding of the term to their reading. So that there can be clarity about my own understanding let me here share the description of Elizabeth Liebert, which captures the "spirit" of my own view: "'Spirituality' connotes

the lived pattern of engaging the presence of the Holy, becoming intimate with the presence of God and letting that presence inform all one's actions. This intimacy arises in the context of the community of faith, within its shared belief system." Elizabeth Liebert, "Biblical Prayer for Preachers (And Other Christians)," in *The Hidden Spirit: Discovering the Spirituality of Institutions*, ed. James F. Cobble, Jr., and Charles M. Elliot (Matthews, NC: Christian Ministry Resources, 1999), 45.

3. Ernest Boyer, Jr., *Finding God at Home: Family Life as a Spiritual Discipline* (San Francisco: Harper and Row, 1988), p. 73.

4. Thomas G. Bandy, *Kicking Habits: Welcome Relief for Addicted Churches, Upgrade Edition* (Nashville: Abingdon Press, 2001), 77.

5. Ibid.

6. Leander Keck, *The Church Confident* (Nashville: Abingdon Press, 1993), 27.

7. Ibid., 30.

8. Ibid., 35.

9. Michael Slaughter, *Out on the Edge: A Wake-Up Call for Church Leaders on the Edge of the Media Reformation* (Nashville: Abingdon Press, 1998), 25.

10. Paul Nixon, *Fling Open the Doors: Giving the Church Away to the Community* (Nashville: Abingdon Press, 2002), 7–8.

11. Gifts and call are also discussed as part of the equipping element of discipleship in chapter 4.

12. 1 Corinthians 12:7–11.

13. Confidence in God's abundant provision, even when it is not readily apparent, is an insight offered by the Feeding of the Five Thousand (Mark 6:35–44).

14. Bandy, *Kicking Habits,* 60.

15. Carlyle Marney, *Priests to Each Other* (Valley Forge, PA: Judson Press, 1974), 9. Marney went on to boldly state that given the current state of affairs the clergy was in fact nothing more than a "kept harlotry," colluding with laity to prostitute the true nature of the church in order to avoid the true nature of priesthood. "We have multiplied institutions and orders and organizations masking the needs behind the robe, the title, and the office: we have increased function and form over relation and redemption, and we do this in order to evade the cat on our own back which is our own priesthood.

The result has been the creation of a schizophrenic ministry that does not know what it is for, and a confused laity being used for the wrong ends." Marney, 10.

16. Marney, *Priests to Each Other*, 14–15.

17. Equipping is one of the three elements of discipleship discussed in chapter 4.

18. C. Jeff Woods, *Congregational Megatrends* (Herndon, VA: Alban Institute, 1996), 135.

19. Lawrence O. Richards and Clyde Hoeldtke, *A Theology of Church Leadership* (Grand Rapids, MI: Zondervan, 1980), 195.

20. Richards and Hoeldtke, 199.

21. Bandy, *Kicking Habits*, 155–162.

22. William M. Easum, *Sacred Cows Make Gourmet Burgers: Ministry Anytime, Anywhere, By Anybody* (Nashville: Abingdon Press, 1995), 131.

23. Bandy, *Kicking Habits*, 151. See also Thomas G. Bandy, *Christian Chaos: Revolutionizing the Congregation* (Nashville: Abingdon Press, 1999), 203–231. When these four dimensions are present in a small group they lead almost inevitably to experiences of deepening, equipping, and ministering. While the perspectives are somewhat different, the result of participation in both sets of experiences will be the forming of disciples.

CHAPTER SEVEN, LEADERSHIP IN THE DISCIPLE-FORMING CONGREGATION

1. Parker Palmer, "Leading from Within: Reflections on Spirituality and Leadership," (Washington, DC: The Servant Leadership School, 1990), 5.

2. Parker Palmer, *The Active Life: A Spirituality of Work, Creativity, and Caring* (San Francisco: Harper and Row, 1990; Jossey-Bass, 1999), 99–119.

3. Ibid., 106.

4. Ibid., 107.

5. Ibid., 111.

6. Ibid., 114.

7. See pages 93–96 of this book.

8. See pages 96–98 of this book.

9. Bill Easum, *Leadership on the Other Side: No Rules, Just Clues* (Nashville, Abingdon Press, 2000), 35.

10. Ibid., 90.

11. Leonard Sweet, *Aquachurch: Essential Leadership Arts for Piloting Your Church in Today's Fluid Culture* (Loveland, CO: Group Publishing, 1999), 19.

12. Thomas G. Bandy, *Kicking Habits: Welcome Relief for Addicted Churches, Upgrade Edition* (Nashville: Abingdon Press, 2001), 174.

13. Help for discerning vision in the congregation can be found in C. Jeff Woods, *Better Than Success: 8 Principles of Faithful Leadership* (Valley Forge, PA: Judson Press, 2001), 1–28, and Thomas G. Bandy, *Moving Off the Map: A Field Guide to Changing the Congregation* (Nashville: Abingdon Press, 1998), 178–199.

14. Sweet, *AquaChurch*, 141.

15. Robert Greenleaf, *Servant Leadership: A Journey into the Nature of Legitimate Power and Greatness* (New York: Paulist Press, 1977), 13.

16. Ibid.

17. Sweet, *AquaChurch*, 39.

18. For a thorough discussion of the role and functions of teams in the life of the congregation see Thomas G. Bandy, *Christian Chaos: Revolutionizing the Congregation* (Nashville: Abingdon Press, 1999).

19. Easum, *Leadership on the Other Side*, 19.

20. Ronald Heifetz, *Leadership Without Easy Answers* (Cambridge, MA, Belknap Press, 1994), 22.

21. Jim Herrington, Mike Bonem, and James H. Furr. *Leading Congregational Change: A Practical Guide for the Transformational Journey* (San Francisco: Jossey-Bass, 2000), 34.

22. See Heifetz, *Leadership Without Easy Answers*, 128ff., for a more complete discussion of these principles.

23. Easum, *Leadership on the Other Side*, 35.

24. Herrington et al., *Leading Congregational Change*, 9.

CHAPTER EIGHT, ENTRY POINTS

1. Charles M. Olsen, *Transforming Church Boards into Communities of Spiritual Leaders* (Herndon, VA: Alban Institute, 1995), 10.

2. Ibid., 76.

3. There are a variety of resources available to help you do this and more are being added regularly. Currently some of the more helpful ones are: *Twelve Keys to an Effective Church* by Kennon

Callahan (Jossey-Bass, 1997), *The Complete Ministry Audit* by Bill Easum (Abingdon Press, 1996), *Facing Reality: A Tool for Congregational Assessment* by Thomas G. Bandy (Abingdon Press, 2001), and *Holy Conversations: Strategic Planning as a Spiritual Practice for Congregations* by Gil Rendle and Alice Mann (Alban Institute, 2003).

CHAPTER NINE, PERSPECTIVES ON A "POST-" WORLD

1. See Margaret Wheatley, *Leadership and the New Science* (San Francisco: Berrett-Koehler, 1999), 121–138, for a discussion of chaos theory.

2. Robert T. Handy, *A Christian America: Protestant Hopes and Historical Realities* (New York: Oxford University Press, 1971), viii.

3. Mead uses the term paradigm to describe the established way of looking at the world and the church that developed during the Age of Christendom and earlier during the Apostolic Age. These characteristics are described in Loren Mead, *The Once and Future Church: Reinventing the Congregation for a New Mission Frontier* (Herndon, VA: Alban Institute, 1991), 15–17.

4. Congregational polity churches have never officially adopted this view of the parish, seeing themselves much more readily as voluntary organizations. Despite this official view, however, they have in a broader sense participated in the general understanding of the church as parish. They, too, have recognized a particular relationship to and role in their communities, in everything from social service efforts to praying at town council meetings. It is not so much an official statement of polity that matters as it is the understanding of the role the church has in relationship to its community and its various civic institutions.

5. Mead, *Once and Future Church,* 18.

6. Ibid.

7. This description of postmodernism follows many of the characteristics suggested in Stanley J. Grenz, *A Primer on Postmodernism* (Grand Rapids, MI: Eerdmans, 1996) and J. Richard Middleton and Brian J. Walsh, *Truth is Stranger Than It Used to Be: Biblical Faith in a Postmodern Age* (Downers Grove, IL: InterVarsity Press, 1995), two books that provide a well-articulated discussion of postmodernism and the challenges it presents to Christian faith and practice.

8. Leonard Sweet, *Post-Modern Pilgrims: First Century Passion for the 21st Century World* (Nashville: Broadman and Holman, 2000), 28.

9. In *Engle v. Vitale* in 1962, the U.S. Supreme Court ruled unconstitutional a prayer written by the New York State Board of Regents. In 1963, in *Abington v. Schempp* and *Murray v. Curlett,* the recitation of the Lord's Prayer and devotional Bible reading were ruled unconstitutional. See F. S. Adeney, "Prayer in Public Schools" in *Dictionary of Christianity in America,* ed. Daniel G. Reid, Robert D. Linder, Bruce L. Shelley, Harry S. Stout (Downers's Grove, IL: InterVarsity Press, 1990), 921.

10. The concept of quest to describe the contemporary spiritual search is found in Wade Clark Roof's *Spiritual Marketplace: Baby Boomers and the Remaking of American Religion* (Princeton, NJ: Princeton University Press, 1999). Although Roof focuses his attention on the Boomer generation and dismisses the notion of postmodernism, many of his insights provide an accurate description of contemporary reality for generations both younger and older than Boomers. See Roof, 46–76.

11. The distinction I wish to draw between mission and ministry is primarily based on whether it is corporate or individual. Mission is the corporate responsibility of the church—in both its congregational and denominational forms. Ministry, on the other hand, is the individual's participation in that mission. This view differs from that which draws the distinction based on the location of the efforts—whether they are within or outside of the church. I resist that form of distinction because I believe it creates an inappropriate dichotomy that has often supported the busy involvement of laity within the church, leaving little time for engagement outside the church. Furthermore, it enhances a "we-they" mentality that has negative consequences for mission in both locations. In some cases "they" are seen as less fortunate and capable and efforts there are condescending. In other cases, "we" are seen as being privileged and efforts there are viewed as selfish. Mission is the work of the church, both internally and externally. Ministry is the involvement of individuals in that mission. This approach affirms and encourages a ministry of the laity and clergy that happens both internally and externally to support the mission of the church.

CHAPTER TEN, A VIEW FROM EXILE

1. Good summaries of the more traditional understanding of the exile experience, which is presented here, are found in Peter R. Ackroyd, *Exile and Restoration: A Study of Hebrew Thought of the Sixth Century B.C.,* The Old Testament Library (Philadelphia: The Westminster Press, 1968) and Ralph W. Klein, *Israel in Exile: A Theological Interpretation,* Overtures to Biblical Theology (Philadelphia: Fortress Press, 1979).

2. At least one other testimony stands beside that of the prophetic view that the exile was God's punishment for Israel's sin. The book of Job, most likely dating in its current form from the early post-exilic period, provides a different perspective. Despite his friends' insistence that his own sin is the cause of his suffering, Job continues to maintain that it is not, that something else must be at work. Many commentators believe that this provides a challenge to the more common argument that Israel's sin is responsible for the exile. These two perspectives stand together in the biblical witness. There is no resolution of their differences. And yet while the perspectives are radically different, each of them maintains a deep concern for faithfulness, especially God's faithfulness to the people. Those who have sinned are called to repentance and a new way of living, because God has remembered them and seeks to bring them home. Those who have suffered for no fault of their own are reminded that God remains a source of comfort even in the midst of chaotic dislocation and unexplained suffering.

3. Key insights regarding Ezekiel's view of the holiness of God are found in Walter Brueggemann, *Hopeful Imagination: Prophetic Voices in Exile* (Philadelphia: Fortress Press, 1986), 49–87.

4. Various writings of Walter Brueggemann suggest the importance of the prophetic role in the expression of rage, providing comfort, and offering hope. These have provided the beginning point for this discussion. See particularly *The Prophetic Imagination* (Philadelphia: Fortress Press, 1978) and *Hopeful Imagination: Prophetic Voices in Exile* (Philadelphia: Fortress Press, 1986).

5. Walter Brueggemann, *Cadences of Home: Preaching Among Exiles* (Louisville: Westminster John Knox, 1997), 1.

❖ Bibliography

BOOKS THAT PROVIDE INSIGHT INTO THE END OF
    CHRISTENDOM
    (CHAPTERS ONE AND NINE)

Cimino, Richard, and Don Lattin. *Shopping for Faith: American Religion in the New Millennium*. San Francisco: Jossey-Bass: 1998.

Clapp, Rodney. *A Peculiar People: The Church as Culture in a Post-Christian Society*. Downer's Grove, IL: InterVarsity Press, 1996.

Guder, Darrell L., ed. *Missional Church: A Vision for the Sending of the Church in North America*. Grand Rapids, MI: Eerdmans, 1998.

Hauerwas, Stanley, and William Willimon. *Resident Aliens: Life in the Christian Colony*. Nashville: Abingdon Press, 1989.

Johnstone, Ronald L. *Religion in Society: A Sociology of Religion*, sixth edition. Upper Saddle River, NJ: Prentice Hall, 2001.

Mead, Loren. *The Once and Future Church: Reinventing the Congregation for a New Mission Frontier*. Herndon, VA: Alban Institute, 1991.

———. *Five Challenges for the Once and Future Church*. Herndon, VA: Alban Institute, 1996.

Newbigin, Lesslie. *The Gospel in a Pluralist Society*. Grand Rapids, MI: Eerdmans, 1989.

Roof, Wade Clark. *Spiritual Marketplace: Baby Boomers and the Remaking of American Religion.* Princeton, NJ: Princeton University Press, 1999.

BOOKS THAT PROVIDE INSIGHT INTO POSTMODERNITY
(CHAPTERS ONE AND NINE)

Beaudoin, Tom. *Virtual Faith: The Irreverent Spiritual Quest of Generation X.* San Francisco: Jossey-Bass, 1998.

Ford, Kevin Graham. *Jesus for a New Generation: Putting the Gospel in the Language of Xers.* Downers Grove, IL: InterVarsity Press, 1995.

Gallup, George Jr., and Timothy Jones. *The Next American Spirituality: Finding God in the Twenty-First Century.* Colorado Springs: Victor, 2000.

Grenz, Stanley. *A Primer on Postmodernism.* Grand Rapids, MI: Eerdmans, 1996.

McLaren, Brian D. *A New Kind of Christian.* San Francisco: Jossey-Bass, 2001.

———. *The Church on the Other Side: Doing Ministry in the Post-Modern Matrix.* Grand Rapids, MI: Zondervan, 2000.

Middleton, J. Richard, and Brian J. Walsh. *Truth is Stranger Than It Used to Be: Biblical Faith in a Postmodern Age.* Downers Grove, IL: InterVarsity Press, 1995.

Sweet, Leonard. *Post-Modern Pilgrims: First Century Passion for the 21st Century World.* Nashville: Broadman and Holman, 2000.

———. *Aquachurch: Essential Leadership Arts for Piloting Your Church in Today's Fluid Culture.* Loveland, CO: Group Publishing, 1999.

Wheatley, Margaret. *Leadership and the New Science.* San Francisco: Barrett-Koehler, 1992.

BOOKS THAT PROVIDE INSIGHT INTO THE MINISTRY OF
JESUS AND THE EARLY CHURCH
(CHAPTER THREE)

Bowker, John. *Jesus and the Pharisees.* Cambridge: Cambridge University Press, 1973.

Bruce, A. B. *The Training of the Twelve.* Edinburgh: T & T Clark, 1871.

Donaldson, Terence L. "Guiding Readers—Making Disciples: Discipleship in Matthew's Narrative Strategy." In *Patterns of Dis-*

cipleship in the New Testament, ed. by Richard N. Longenecker, 30-49. Grand Rapids, MI: Eerdmans, 1996.

Haenchen, Ernest. *The Acts of the Apostles: A Commentary,* trans. B. Noble et al. Philadelphia: Westminster Press, 1971.

Hurtado, Larry W. "Following Jesus in the Gospel of Mark – and Beyond." In *Patterns of Discipleship in the New Testament,* ed. Richard N. Longenecker, 9-29. Grand Rapids, MI: Eerdmans, 1996.

Johnson, Luke Timothy. *The Acts of the Apostles,* Sacra Pagina Series, vol. 5. Collegeville, MN: The Liturgical Press, 1992.

Kern, Kathleen. *We Are the Pharisees.* Scottdale: Herald Press, 1995.

Longenecker, Richard N. "Taking Up the Cross Daily: Discipleship in Luke-Acts." In *Patterns of Discipleship in the New Testament,* ed. by Richard N. Longenecker, 50-76. Grand Rapids, MI: Eerdmans, 1996.

Marshall, Alfred. *The RSV Interlinear Greek-English New Testament.* Grand Rapids, MI: Zondervan, 1958.

Parker, Harold M., Jr. "The Great Commission," *Interpretation,* Vol. 2, No. 1 (January 1948) : 74-75.

Simon, Marcel. *Jewish Sects at the Time of Jesus.* Philadelphia: Fortress Press, 1967.

Stemberger, Gunter. *Jewish Contemporaries of Jesus: Pharisees, Sadducees, Essenes.* Translated by Allan W. Mahnke. Minneapolis: Fortress Press, 1995.

Sweetland, Dennis M. *Our Journey with Jesus: Discipleship according to Luke-Acts.* Good News Studies 23. Collegeville, MN: The Liturgical Press, 1990

Wall, Robert W. "The Acts of the Apostles," *The New Interpreter's Bible,* Vol. X. Nashville: Abingdon Press, 2002.

Willimon, William H. *Acts.* Interpretation: A Biblical Commentary for Teaching and Preaching. Atlanta: John Knox Press, 1988.

BOOKS THAT PROVIDE INSIGHT INTO DISCIPLESHIP
(CHAPTERS THREE AND FOUR)

Aleshire, Daniel O. *Faithcare: Ministering to All God's People through the Ages of Life.* Philadelphia: Westminster Press, 1988.

Barna, George. *Growing True Disciples.* Ventura, CA: Issachar Resources, 2000.

Bonhoeffer, Dietrich. *The Cost of Discipleship*, revised edition. London: SCM Press, 1959; New York: MacMillan Publishing, 1963.

———. *Life Together.* New York: Harper and Row, 1954.

Boyer, Ernest, Jr. *Finding God at Home: Family Life as a Spiritual Discipline.* San Francisco: Harper and Row, 1988.

Cosgrove, Francis M. Jr. *Essentials of Discipleship: Practical Help on How to Live as Christ's Disciple.* Colorado Springs: NavPress, 1980.

Eims, Leroy. *The Lost Art of Disciple Making.* Grand Rapids, MI: Zondervan, 1978.

Foster, Richard. *Celebration of Discipline: The Path to Spiritual Growth.* New York: Harper and Row, 1978.

Fowler, James W. *Becoming Adult, Becoming Christian: Adult Development and Christian Faith.* San Francisco: Jossey-Bass, 2000.

Hull, Bill. *The Disciple-Making Church.* Grand Rapids, MI: Fleming H. Revell, 1990.

———. *The Disciple-Making Pastor.* Grand Rapids, MI: Fleming H. Revell, 1988.

Johnson, Susanne. *Christian Spiritual Formation in the Church and Classroom.* Nashville: Abingdon Press, 1989.

Jones, Jeffrey D. *Youth Ministry: Making and Shaping Disciples.* Valley Forge, PA: Judson Press, 1986.

Kelsey, Morton. "Educating Children Spiritually and Psychologically." *Religious Education,* vol. 89, no. 4 (Fall 1994): 530–540.

Loder, James E. *The Logic of the Spirit: Human Development in Theological Perspective.* San Francisco: Jossey-Bass, 1998.

Marney, Carlyle. *Priests to Each Other.* Valley Forge, PA: Judson Press, 1974.

Palmer, Parker. *The Active Life: A Spirituality of Work, Creativity, and Caring.* San Francisco: Harper and Row, 1990; Jossey Bass, 1999.

———. *The Courage to Teach: Exploring the Inner Landscape of the Teacher's Life.* San Francisco: Jossey-Bass, 1998.

Pazmiño, Robert W. *God Our Teacher: Theological Basics in Christian Education.* Grand Rapids, MI: Baker Academic, 2001.

Ware, Corrine. *Discover Your Spiritual Type: A Guide to Individual and Congregational Growth.* Herndon, VA: Alban Institute, 1995.

Westerhoff, John. *Spiritual Life: The Foundation for Preaching and Teaching.* Louisville: Westminster John Knox, 1994.

Wink, Walter. *Engaging the Power: Discernment and Resistance in a World of Domination.* Minneapolis: Augsburg Fortress, 1992.

Books That Provide Insight into the Congregation
as It Forms Disciples
(chapters five and six)

Bandy, Thomas G. *Kicking Habits: Welcome Relief for Addicted Churches,* upgrade edition. Nashville: Abingdon Press, 2001.

———. *Christian Chaos: Revolutionizing the Congregation.* Nashville: Abingdon Press, 1999.

———. *Facing Reality: A Tool for Congregational Assessment.* Nashville: Abingdon Press, 2001.

———. *Moving Off the Map: A Field Guide to Changing the Congregation.* Nashville: Abingdon Press, 1998.

Barna, George. *Habits of Highly Effective Churches,* Ventura, CA: Regal Books, 1999.

Bass, Diana Butler. *The Practicing Congregation: Imagining a New Old Church.* Herndon, VA: Alban Institute, 2004.

Bass, Dorothy C, ed. *Practicing Our Faith,* San Francisco: Jossey-Bass, 1997.

Callahan, Kennon L. *Dynamic Worship.* San Francisco: Jossey Bass, 1994.

———. *Twelve Keys to an Effective Church.* San Francisco: Jossey Bass, 1997.

Cladis, George. *Leading the Team Based Church: How Pastors and Church Staffs Can Grow Together into a Powerful Fellowship of Leaders.* San Francisco: Jossey-Bass, 1999.

Cobble, James F. and Charles M. Eliott, ed. *The Hidden Spirit: Discovering the Spirituality of Institutions.* Matthews, NC: Christian Ministry Resources, 1999.

Dawn, Marva J. *Reaching Out without Dumbing Down: A Theology of Worship for This Urgent Time.* Grand Rapids, MI: Eerdmans, 1995.

Dykstra, Craig. *Growing in the Life of Faith: Education and the Christian Practices.* Louisville: Geneva Press, 1999.

Easum, William. *Dancing with Dinosaurs: Ministry in a Hostile and Hurting World*. Nashville: Abingdon Press, 1993.

————. *The Complete Ministry Audit*. Nashville, Abingdon Press, 1996.

————. *Sacred Cows Make Gourmet Burgers*. Nashville: Abingdon Press, 1995.

Easum, William and Thomas G. Bandy. *Growing Spiritual Redwoods*. Nashville Abingdon Press, 1997.

Keck, Leander. *The Church Confident*. Nashville: Abingdon Press, 1993.

Nixon, Paul. *Fling Open the Doors: Giving the Church Away to the Community*. Nashville: Abingdon Press, 2002.

Olsen, Charles M. *Transforming Church Board into Communities of Spiritual Leaders*. Herndon, VA: Alban Institute, 1995.

Pagitt, Doug. *Reimagining Church: A Week in the Life of an Experimental Church*. El Cajon, CA: emergent YS Books, 2004.

Payne, Claude E., and Hamilton Beazley. *Reclaiming the Great Commission: A Practical Model for Transforming Denominations and Congregations*. San Francisco: Jossey-Bass, 2000.

Rendle, Gil, and Alice Mann. *Holy Conversations: Strategic Planning as a Spiritual Practice for Congregations*. Herndon, VA: Alban Institute, 2003.

Schwartz, Christian A. *Natural Church Development*. Carol Stream, IL: ChurchSmart Resources, 1997.

————. *The Three Colors of Ministry: A Trinitarian Approach to Identifying and Developing Gifts*. St. Charles, IL: ChurchSmart Resources, 2001.

Schwartz, Christian A. and Christoph Schalk. *Implementation Guide to Natural Church Development*. Carol Stream, IL: ChurchSmart Resources, 1998.

Slaughter, Michael. *Out on the Edge: A Wake-Up Call for Church Leaders on the Edge of the Media Reformation*. Nashville: Abingdon Press, 1998.

Stevens, R. Paul and Phil Collins. *The Equipping Pastor: A Systems Approach to Congregational Leadership*. Herndon, VA: Alban Institute: 1993.

Woods, C. Jeff. *Congregational Megatrends*. Herndon, VA: Alban Institute, 1996.

Books That Provide Insight into Leadership (chapter seven)

Bandy, Thomas G. *Coaching Change: Breaking Down Resistance, Building Up Hope*. Nashville: Abingdon Press, 2000.

DePree, Max. *Leadership is an Art*. New York: Doubleday, 1989.

———. *Leadership Jazz*. New York: Doubleday, 1992.

Easum, Bill. *Leadership on the Other Side*. Nashville: Abingdon Press, 2000.

Fulan, Michael. *Leading in a Culture of Change*. San Francisco: Jossey-Bass, 2001.

Greenleaf, Robert. *Servant Leadership: A Journey into the Nature of Legitimate Power and Greatness*. New York: Paulist Press, 1977.

———. *The Power of Servant Leaderhip*. San Francisco: Berrett-Koehler, 1998.

Heifetz, Ronald. *Leadership Without Easy Answers*. Cambridge, MA: Belknap Press, 1994.

Herrington, Jim, Mike Bonem, and James H. Furr. *Leading Congregational Change: A Practical Guide for the Transformational Journey*. San Francisco: Jossey-Bass, 2000.

Kotter, John P. *Leading Change*. Boston: Harvard Business School Press, 1996.

Richards, Lawrence O. and Clyde Hoeldtke. *A Theology of Church Leadership*. Grand Rapids, MI: Zondervan, 1980.

Woods, C. Jeff. *Better Than Success: 8 Principles of Faithful Leadership*. Valley Forge, PA: Judson Press, 2001.

Books That Provide Insight into the Exile (chapter ten)

Ackroyd, Peter R. *Exile and Restoration: A Study of Hebrew Thought of the Sixth Century B.C.* The Old Testament Library. Philadelphia: Westminster Press, 1968.

Brueggemann, Walter. *Cadences of Home: Preaching Among Exiles*. Louisville: Westminster John Knox, 1997.

———. *Old Testament Theology*. Minneapolis: Fortress Press, 1992.

———. *Hopeful Imagination: Prophetic Voices in Exile*. Minneapolis: Fortress Press, 1986.

————. *The Prophetic Imagination* (Philadelphia: Fortress Press, 1978).

————. *Theology of the Old Testament: Testimony, Dispute, Advocacy* Minneapolis: Fortress Press, 1997.

Grabbe, Lester L., ed. *Leading Captivity Captive: "The Exile" as History and Ideology, Journal for the Study of the Old Testament,* Supplement Series 278. European Seminar in Historical Methodology 2. Sheffield: Sheffield Academic Press, 1998.

Klein, Ralph W. *Israel in Exile: A Theological Interpretation.* Overtures to Biblical Theology. Philadelphia: Fortress Press, 1979.

Newsom, Carol A. "The Book of Job: Introduction, Commentary, and Reflections," *The New Interpreter's Bible,* vol. 4. Nashville: Abingdon Press, 1996.

Additional Permissions Acknowledgements